BAPTISTWAY ADULT BIBLE STUDY GUIDE®

Psalms
SONGS FROM THE HEART OF FAITH

VIVIAN CONRAD
RON LYLES
DON RANEY
BYRON STEVENSON
MEREDITH STONE

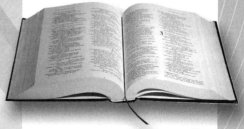

BAPTISTWAYPRESS®
Dallas, Texas

Psalms: Songs from the Heart of Faith—BaptistWay Adult Bible Study Guide®

BAPTISTWAY PRESS® Leadership Team
Executive Director, Baptist General Convention of Texas: David Hardage
Director, Education/Discipleship Center: Chris Liebrum
Director, Bible Study/Discipleship Team: Phil Miller
Publisher, BaptistWay Press®: Scott Stevens

Publishing consultant and editor: Ross West
Cover and Interior Design and Production: Desktop Miracles, Inc.
Printing: Data Reproductions Corporation

First edition: March 2013
ISBN–13: 978–1–931060–04–2

How to Make the Best Use of This Issue

Whether you're the teacher or a student—

1. Start early in the week before your class meets.

2. Overview the study. Review the table of contents and read the study introduction. Try to see how each lesson relates to the overall study.

3. Use your Bible to read and consider prayerfully the Scripture passages for the lesson. (You'll see that each writer has chosen a favorite translation for the lessons in this issue. You're free to use the Bible translation you prefer and compare it with the translation chosen for that unit, of course.)

4. After reading all the Scripture passages in your Bible, then read the writer's comments. The comments are intended to be an aid to your study of the Bible.

5. Read the small articles—"sidebars"—in each lesson. They are intended to provide additional, enrichment information and inspiration and to encourage thought and application.

6. Try to answer for yourself the questions included in each lesson. They're intended to encourage further thought and application, and they can also be used in the class session itself.

If you're the teacher—

A. Do all of the things just mentioned, of course. As you begin the study with your class, be sure to find a way to help your class know the date on which each lesson will be studied. You might do this in one or more of the following ways:

   • In the first session of the study, briefly overview the study by identifying with your class the date on which each lesson will be studied. Lead your class to write the date in the table of contents on page 9 and on the first page of each lesson.

- Make and post a chart that indicates the date on which each lesson will be studied.

- If all of your class has e-mail, send them an e-mail with the dates the lessons will be studied.

- Provide a bookmark with the lesson dates. You may want to include information about your church and then use the bookmark as an outreach tool, too. A model for a bookmark can be downloaded from www.baptistwaypress.org on the Resources for Adults page.

- Develop a sticker with the lesson dates, and place it on the table of contents or on the back cover.

B. Get a copy of the *Teaching Guide*, a companion piece to this *Study Guide*. The *Teaching Guide* contains additional Bible comments plus two teaching plans. The teaching plans in the *Teaching Guide* are intended to provide practical, easy-to-use teaching suggestions that will work in your class.

C. After you've studied the Bible passage, the lesson comments, and other material, use the teaching suggestions in the *Teaching Guide* to help you develop your plan for leading your class in studying each lesson.

D. Teaching resource items for use as handouts are available free at www.baptistwaypress.org.

E. You may want to get the additional adult Bible study comments— *Adult Online Bible Commentary*—by Dr. Jim Denison (president, Denison Forum on Truth and Culture, and theologian-in-residence, Baptist General Convention of Texas). Call 1–866–249–1799 or e-mail baptistway@texasbaptists.org to order *Adult Online Bible Commentary*. It is available only in electronic format (PDF) from our website, www.baptistwaypress.org. The price of these comments for the entire study is $6 for individuals and $25 for a group of five. A church or class that participates in our advance order program for free shipping can receive *Adult Online Bible Commentary* free. Call 1–866–249–1799 or see www.baptistwaypress.org to purchase or for information on participating in our free shipping program for the next study.

F. Additional teaching plans are also available in electronic format (PDF) by calling 1–866–249–1799. The price of these additional teaching plans for the entire study is $5 for an individual and $20 for a group of five. A church or class that participates in our advance order program for free shipping can receive *Adult Online Teaching Plans* free. Call 1–866–249–1799 or see www.baptistwaypress.org for information on participating in our free shipping program for the next study.

G. You also may want to get the enrichment teaching help that is provided on the internet by the *Baptist Standard* at www.baptiststandard.com. (Other class participants may find this information helpful, too.) Call 214–630–4571 to begin your subscription to the electronic edition of the *Baptist Standard*.

H. Enjoy leading your class in discovering the meaning of the Scripture passages and in applying these passages to their lives.

Note: The time of the first release of these materials includes Easter. To meet the needs of churches who wish to have a Bible study lesson specifically on the Easter Scripture passages at this time, an Easter lesson is included.

DO YOU USE A KINDLE?

This BaptistWay *Adult Bible Study Guide* plus *Living Generously for Jesus' Sake; Profiles in Character; Amos, Hosea, Isaiah, Micah; The Gospel of Matthew; The Gospel of Mark; The Gospel of John: Part One; The Gospel of John: Part Two; The Book of Acts: Time to Act on Acts 1:8;* and *The Corinthian Letters: Imperatives for an Imperfect Church* are now available in a Kindle edition. The easiest way to find these materials is to search for "BaptistWay" on your Kindle or go to www.amazon.com/kindle and do a search for "BaptistWay." The Kindle edition can be studied not only on a Kindle but also on a PC, Mac, iPhone, iPad, Blackberry, or Android phone using the Kindle app available free from amazon.com/kindle.

AUDIO BIBLE STUDY LESSONS

Do you want to use your walk/run/ride, etc. time to study the Bible? Or maybe you're a college student who wants to listen to the lesson on your iPod®? Or maybe you're looking for a way to study the Bible when you just can't find time to read? Or maybe you know someone who has difficulty seeing to read even our *Large Print Study Guide*?

Then try our audio Bible study lessons, available on *Living Generously for Jesus' Sake*; *Profiles in Character*; *Amos, Hosea, Isaiah, Micah*; *The Gospel of Matthew*; *The Gospel of Mark*; *The Gospel of Luke*; *The Gospel of John: Part One*; *The Gospel of John: Part Two*; *The Book of Acts*; *The Corinthian Letters*; *Galatians and 1 & 2 Thessalonians*; and *The Letters of James and John*. For more information or to order, call 1–866–249–1799 or e-mail baptistway@texasbaptists.org. The files are downloaded from our website. You'll need an audio player that plays MP3 files (like an iPod®, but many MP3 players are available), or you can listen on a computer.

Writers for This Study Guide

Meredith Stone wrote lessons one and two. Rev. Stone serves as Women in Ministry Specialist for Texas Baptists. Meredith has taught adjunctively for Hardin-Simmons University in the areas of Old Testament and Hebrew. She is a graduate of Hardin-Simmons (B.A., M.A.) and is working toward a Ph.D. in Biblical Interpretation at Brite Divinity School, Fort Worth, Texas.

Byron Stevenson wrote lesson three and the Easter lesson. He is senior pastor of The Fort Bend Church in Sugar Land, Texas. He is a graduate of Southern University, Baton Rouge, Louisiana, with a Bachelor of Science in Accounting, and he also earned a Masters of Arts in Theological Studies degree from Houston Baptist University. He was elected first vice president of the Baptist General Convention of Texas in 2012.

Ron Lyles, writer of lessons four through seven, has been the pastor of the South Main Baptist Church of Pasadena, Texas, for more than thirty years. He has also been writing Bible study material for most of that time. Dr. Lyles is a graduate of Dallas Baptist University and Southwestern Baptist Theological Seminary (M.Div., Ph.D.). He also enjoys teaching adjunctively for Logsdon Seminary at their Corpus Christi location.

Don Raney wrote lessons eight through ten. Dr. Raney is pastor of First Baptist Church, Petersburg, Texas. Don has taught as an adjunct for Southwestern Baptist Theological Seminary, Texas Christian University, Mid-America Christian University, and Wayland Baptist University. He is a graduate of the University of Alabama (B.A.) and received his Ph.D. in Old Testament from Southwestern Baptist Theological Seminary.

Vivian Conrad wrote lessons eleven through thirteen in the *Adult Bible Study Guide* and the accompanying teaching plans in the *Adult*

Bible Teaching Guide. After teaching Old Testament and biblical studies for twelve years at an international Christian school in the Philippines, she now serves as executive director of Mineral Wells Senior Center, Mineral Wells, Texas. She holds degrees in Christian Education and Theology from Dallas Baptist University and Southwestern Baptist Theological Seminary. Vivian and her husband are active in the music and teaching ministry of Clear Fork Baptist Church in Azle, Texas.

Psalms: Songs from the Heart of Faith

How to Make the Best Use of This Issue   3
Writers for This Study Guide   7
Introducing Psalms: Songs from the Heart of Faith   11

DATE OF STUDY

LESSON 1 _____   *Lord of All*
                      PSALMS 2; 110   15

LESSON 2 _____   *God's Majestic Greatness*
                      PSALM 8   25

LESSON 3 _____   *It's a Wonderful Life*
                      PSALM 16   33

LESSON 4 _____   *Trusting God in the Darkest Hour*
                      PSALM 22   41

LESSON 5 _____   *Committed to the Lord*
                      PSALM 31   51

LESSON 6 _____   *The Joy of Forgiveness*
                      PSALM 32   61

LESSON 7 _____   *Desiring Life and Finding Its Source*
                      PSALM 34   71

LESSON 8 _____   *Gratitude for God's Help*
                      PSALM 40   81

LESSON 9 _____   *No One Does Good*
                      PSALM 53   91

LESSON 10 _____   *A Desperate Cry*
                      PSALM 69   99

LESSON 11 _____   *Testifying of God's Security and Deliverance*
                      PSALM 91   109

LESSON 12 _____   *Let Us Worship, Let Us Obey*
                      PSALM 95   119

LESSON 13 _____   *Give Thanks for the Lord's Steadfast Love*
                        PSALM 118   129

EASTER   _____   *Experiencing, Believing, Telling*
LESSON   JOHN 20:1–18   139

Our Next New Study   149
How to Order More Bible Study Materials   151

Introducing

PSALMS: *Songs from the Heart of Faith*

Psalms? Such nice, sweet songs. What can we learn from them, anyway?

Beware of shortchanging the Book of Psalms. Psalms is an intense, passionate presentation of many if not all of the themes in Old Testament faith. Furthermore, the early church turned to Psalms to authenticate and enhance their faith in Jesus.

For one thing, the early church used the Psalms to enhance its worship experiences. Paul enjoined the Colossians, "Let the word of Christ richly dwell within you, with all wisdom teaching and admonishing one another with psalms and hymns and spiritual songs, singing with thankfulness in your hearts to God" (Colossians 3:16; see also Ephesians 3:19).[1] The strongest likelihood is that "psalms" in both the Colossians and the Ephesians passages refers to the psalms in the Old Testament Book of Psalms. Early Christians with a Jewish background would already have known and sung those psalms.

Perhaps of more significance, the early church also used the Psalms to guide and enrich their theological understanding of who Jesus is and what the Christian faith is all about. The importance of the Book of Psalms to the early church can be seen in that the New Testament quotes Psalms more often than it quotes any other Old Testament book. In addition to actual quotes, Bible scholars can trace many more allusions—ideas and images, not necessarily exact words—in the New Testament to the Psalms.

Approaching the Psalms

This study, *Psalms: Songs from the Heart of Faith,* will provide opportunities both to reflect on the Psalms in their Old Testament context and also to take note of how early Christians made use of them. Both opportunities are important, and both must be used with care. As someone has suggested about studying the Bible, *A text without a context is only a pretext.* Good Bible study calls for studying Scripture in its context rather than imposing one's own context on it in order to promote one's own interpretation. So, in addition to and in light of the Old Testament context for the psalms in this study, the intent in this study is also to see what our fellow Christians in the context of the early years of the church saw in these psalms. Along the way and as a result, we will see important, meaningful applications for our own lives, our own faith.

The psalms in this study have been selected because various New Testament books quote them, using verses from the Psalms to verify, illustrate, and enhance the meaning of the gospel. This study focuses on the psalms that are quoted most often in the New Testament.[2] In the case of psalms in which a similar number of New Testament quotations occurs, psalms that dealt with different subject matter have been chosen.

Hearing from God and Speaking to God

The Book of Psalms is both God's message to God's people and the people's response to God's message. As we study these psalms, let us listen for God's message, and let us also learn from how our spiritual forebears responded.

The Book of Psalms may well be the most read and most influential book in the Old Testament, and its use in the New Testament affirms that thought. So, as we study this book, we join a vast company of believers who have been blessed by it. Too, let us keep in mind both uses for the Book of Psalms—to hear God's message with our own ears and to respond to God with our own voices and lives.

The twentieth-century Christian theologian and martyr Dietrich Bonhoeffer wrote these words about the importance of the Psalms: "Whenever the Psalter is abandoned, an incomparable treasure is lost to the Christian church. With its recovery will come unexpected power."[3]

Let it be so, and let it begin with us and in this study.

Note: Since Easter occurs during the time of the first release of this study, an Easter lesson is provided.

PSALMS: SONGS FROM THE HEART OF FAITH

Lesson 1	Lord of All	Psalms 2; 110
Lesson 2	God's Majestic Greatness	Psalm 8
Lesson 3	It's a Wonderful Life	Psalm 16
Lesson 4	Trusting God in the Darkest Hour	Psalm 22
Lesson 5	Committed to the Lord	Psalm 31
Lesson 6	The Joy of Forgiveness	Psalm 32
Lesson 7	Desiring Life and Finding Its Source	Psalm 34
Lesson 8	Gratitude for God's Help	Psalm 40
Lesson 9	No One Does Good	Psalm 53
Lesson 10	A Desperate Cry	Psalm 69
Lesson 11	Testifying of God's Security and Deliverance	Psalm 91
Lesson 12	Let Us Worship, Let Us Obey	Psalm 95
Lesson 13	Give Thanks for the Lord's Steadfast Love	Psalm 118

Additional Resources for Studying the Book of Psalms[4]

G. K. Beale and D. A. Carson, eds. *Commentary on the New Testament Use of the Old Testament.* Grand Rapids, Michigan: Baker Academic, 2007.

W. H. Bellinger, Jr. *Psalms: Reading and Studying the Book of Praises.* Peabody, Massachusetts: Hendrickson Publishers, 1990.

W. H. Bellinger, Jr. *The Testimony of Poets and Sages: The Psalms and Wisdom Literature.* Macon, Georgia: Smyth and Helwys Publishing, Inc., 1997.

Dietrich Bonhoeffer. *Prayerbook of the Bible* in *Dietrich Bonhoeffer Works*, volume 5. English edition edited by Geffrey B. Kelley and translated by Daniel W. Bloesch and James H. Burtness. Minneapolis, Minnesota: Augsburg Fortress, 2005 (originally published in German in 1987).

Walter Brueggemann. *The Message of the Psalms: A Theological Commentary*. Minneapolis, Minnesota: Augsburg Publishing House, 1984, Kindle edition.

Nancy L. deClaissé-Walford. *Introduction to the Psalms: A Song from Ancient Israel*. St. Louis, Missouri: Chalice Press, 2004.

John I. Durham, "Psalms," *The Broadman Bible Commentary*. Volume 4. Nashville, Tennessee: Broadman Press, 1971.

J. Clinton McCann, Jr. "Psalms." *The New Interpreter's Bible*. Volume 4. Nashville: Abingdon Press, 1996.

James Luther Mays. *Psalms*. Interpretation: A Bible Commentary for Teaching and Preaching. Louisville, Kentucky: John Knox Press, 1994.

Marvin E. Tate. *Psalms 51—100*. Word Biblical Commentary. Waco, Texas: Word, 1990.

NOTES

1. Unless otherwise indicated, all Scripture quotations in "Introducing Psalms: Songs from the Heart of Faith," lesson 3, and the Easter lesson are from the New American Standard Bible (1995 edition).

2. BaptistWay Press also provides a briefer study of the Book of Psalms that takes a different approach in its development. See www.baptistwaypress.org for *Psalms and Proverbs: Songs and Sayings of Faith*.

3. Dietrich Bonhoeffer, *Prayerbook of the Bible* in *Dietrich Bonhoeffer Works*, volume 5, English edition edited by Geffrey B. Kelley and translated by Daniel W. Bloesch and James H. Burtness (Minneapolis, Minnesota: Augsburg Fortress, 2005), 116–117.

4. Listing a book does not imply full agreement by the writers or BAPTISTWAY PRESS® with all of its comments.

LESSON ONE
Lord of All

FOCAL TEXT
Psalms 2; 110

BACKGROUND
Psalms 2; 110

MAIN IDEA
All who oppose the Lord do so in vain, for the Lord reigns over all.

QUESTION TO EXPLORE
Who's in charge here—and everywhere?

STUDY AIM
To acknowledge God's lordship in my life

QUICK READ
Psalms 2 and 110 are royal psalms, which celebrate the Davidic king as the instrument of God's power over all. The Davidic Messiah, Jesus, has lordship over all.

Have you ever been in an electricity blackout that lasted more than a few minutes? Normally when the power is out for just a few minutes, we don't realize the impact. We probably spend those several minutes looking for flashlights. But when the power stays off for a while, we recognize the extreme influence it has on the way we live. The air conditioner goes off, the refrigerator loses coolness, the television and the computer don't work, and we have to carry flashlights just to get to different parts of the house. Although electricity affects virtually every aspect of our lives, it is an unseen power that often goes unnoticed.

Similarly, God is also an unseen power in life who goes unnoticed. Psalms 2 and 110 are meant to remind their readers, or singers, of the unmatched power of God over all of life. They are royal psalms related to a celebration of Israel's kings, but both also emphasize that the rule of those kings is representative of God's own reigning power.[1]

PSALM 2

1 Why do the nations conspire
        and the peoples plot in vain?
2 The kings of the earth take their stand
        and the rulers gather together
    against the LORD
        and against his Anointed One.
3 "Let us break their chains," they say,
        "and throw off their fetters."
4 The One enthroned in heaven laughs;
        the Lord scoffs at them.
5 Then he rebukes them in his anger
        and terrifies them in his wrath, saying,
6 "I have installed my King
        on Zion, my holy hill."
7 I will proclaim the decree of the LORD:
    He said to me, "You are my Son;
        today I have become your Father.
8 Ask of me,
        and I will make the nations your inheritance,
        the ends of the earth your possession.

9 You will rule them with an iron scepter;
 you will dash them to pieces like pottery."
10 Therefore, you kings, be wise;
 be warned, you rulers of the earth.
11 Serve the LORD with fear
 and rejoice with trembling.
12 Kiss the Son, lest he be angry
 and you be destroyed in your way,
 for his wrath can flare up in a moment.
 Blessed are all who take refuge in him.

PSALM 110

Of David. A psalm.
1 The LORD says to my Lord:
 "Sit at my right hand
 until I make your enemies
 a footstool for your feet."
2 The LORD will extend your mighty scepter from Zion;
 you will rule in the midst of your enemies.
3 Your troops will be willing
 on your day of battle.
 Arrayed in holy majesty,
 from the womb of the dawn
 you will receive the dew of your youth.
4 The LORD has sworn
 and will not change his mind:
 "You are a priest forever,
 in the order of Melchizedek."
5 The Lord is at your right hand;
 he will crush kings on the day of his wrath.
6 He will judge the nations, heaping up the dead
 and crushing the rulers of the whole earth.
7 He will drink from a brook beside the way;
 therefore he will lift up his head.

Quotations of Psalms 2 and 110 in the New Testament

Psalm 2—Acts 4:25–26; 13:33; Hebrews 1:5; 5:5;
Revelation 2:26–27; 11:18; 12:5; 19:15
Psalm 110—Matthew 22:44; 26:64; Mark 12:36; 14:62;
Luke 20:42–43; 22:69; Acts 2:34–35;
Hebrews 1:13; 5:6; 7:17, 21

Rebellion and Response (2:1–6)

Neither Psalm 1 nor Psalm 2 has a heading or indication of authorship. Because of their lack of these features, commentators have suggested that the two psalms acted as an introduction to the rest of the Psalter. In its original context, Psalm 2 likely was used as a part of the ceremony that would celebrate the enthronement of a new king. While honoring the new king and his reign, the psalm also emphasized that the king functioned as the instrument of God. The power of God in the world is an important theme that is found throughout the songs of Israel's worship.

Psalm 2:1–3 describes a kind of international conspiracy against God. The nations were plotting against God, with all of the kings gathered together trying to figure out how they could break away from the rule of the Lord and his anointed. The anointed one referred to here is Israel's king. The imaginary group of nations felt as though the Lord and his king had them bound in chains and shackles, and they desired to get free.

God responded to their conspiracy in Psalm 2:4–6. By referring to God as the "the One enthroned in heaven" (Psalm 2:4), the psalmist emphasized God's kingship and power. The ultimate King laughed and scoffed at the nations who were trying to plot against him. No alliance of human powers can ever match the power of the One in heaven, and thus God did not even take the plot seriously. God's laughter then turned to rebukes, and his anger and wrath terrified the nations.

But rather than issuing a divine punishment or judgment on the nations, God merely made a statement to the nations that he had installed his king on Zion, his holy mountain (Ps. 2:6). The simple presence of the Lord's instrument of power was sufficient to level the nations' conspiracy. But the king was not installed just anywhere; the king was on

Zion, the holy mountain. Zion becomes one of the names for Jerusalem in the Old Testament. That Zion is designated as God's "holy" mountain means that it is set apart to belong specifically to God and to be used especially for God's service. The place where the king dwells is the place where God is present and at work. The holy mountain is the place where the king mediates the power of God.

The Kingly Covenant and a Warning (2:7–12)

Now the king moved to the forefront and spoke. The king declared God's covenant with the Davidic kings—that God would be their father and that they would be sons of God. When God established a covenant with David that David's house and kingdom would endure before the Lord forever, God specifically outlined this father-son relationship with the Davidic kings (see 2 Samuel 7:14).

As God's son, the king was subject to an inheritance. The inheritance God promised was "the nations" and "the ends of the earth" (Ps. 2:8). Territorial expansion, having more land and resources, was a concern of every king, and so the promise of all the nations and the ends of the earth meant great power. The king is said to conquer the nations so intently that they are broken and shattered into pieces like a pot that has been smashed with an iron rod.

Then, because of this promise of great power to God's king, the kings of the nations are warned to watch out. If the nations served the Lord, celebrated his rule, and honored God's son the king, they would be saved. If not, they would become like the shattered pot. Thus they are reminded, "Blessed are all who take refuge in him" (2:12). Only those who were sheltered by God's king would find God's blessing.

From an historical perspective, the Davidic dynasty never achieved the world dominance that this psalm suggests. Even at its peak, Israel was a small nation in comparison to the world powers existing all around it. But in its context, the psalm represented God's promise of his power at work in the world through the Davidic king. However, as the monarchy decreased in power, the psalm began to be interpreted in new ways. The exilic community, which existed as a kingless colony of Persia and later other empires, saw this psalm as a promise of the restoration of Israel through a new king in the line of David—a messiah. The New

> ## SON OF GOD
>
> Because of God's promise in the Davidic covenant (see 2 Sam. 7:12–15), the Davidic kings were thought of as *sons of God*. When Jesus is called the Son of God in the New Testament, it may be this connotation of the Davidic king to which the authors were alluding. Being called a *son of God* was another way of being called the Davidic Messiah. So while we often think of a familial, or even biological, relationship when Jesus is called the Son of God, it is likely that the initial audience of the New Testament heard this phrase as a reference to Jesus' role as Messiah and the promise of national Jewish restoration instead of it being an indication of Jesus' divine nature.

Testament then took this interpretation a step further and began to see Jesus as the Son of God represented in the psalm.

At the Lord's Right Hand (Psalm 110)

The heading of Psalm 110, "Of David. A psalm," was a later addition to the psalm. Scholars are divided over the dating of this psalm and its original context. Some say that the psalm belonged to a period during the Davidic monarchy and possibly was a psalm celebrating one of David's victories. Others suggest a later date for the psalm, when the offices of king and priest were more closely related than in David's day. Either way, as with Psalm 2, Psalm 110 also proclaims the Lord's great power as enacted through the king, and subsequent interpretation of the psalm has connected its themes to that of the Messiah and to Jesus.

In Psalm 110:1, the Lord spoke to the king and told him to sit at the Lord's right hand. Sitting in such a place of honor was symbolic of the idea that the king functioned as co-regent with God, or as God's associate. For the king to sit at God's right hand emphasized that it was God who had the ultimate power to conquer enemies. Although the king was the visible face of power, God was the real power even though he was not seen. God was the power through whom the king would extend his "mighty scepter" (Ps. 110:2), "crush kings" (110:5), and "judge the nations" (110:6). What God would enable the king to do in 110:7 is uncertain, for the translation of the Hebrew phrase is unclear. However, the basic meaning of 110:7 appears to suggest that the king would be eternally refreshed and empowered by God's provisions of water so that he could lift up his head and do God's work.

In addition to the celebration of God's power through the king, a unique statement is made of the king, "You are a priest forever, in the order of Melchizedek" (110:4). The Davidic kings did not come from the line of Levi, Moses, or Aaron, and so they should not have had any right to serve the function of priest. However, the psalmist drew on the example of Melchizedek, who blessed Abraham in Genesis 14:18. Melchizedek was the king of Salem (the previous name for Jerusalem), who also functioned as a priest of the Most High God. So, in the Davidic king's home in the new Salem, Jerusalem, God designated that like Melchizedek the king would become a priestly mediator between God and the people.

Psalm 110:1 is the Old Testament passage most frequently quoted in the New Testament. One example is how Jesus used the verse to demonstrate to the Pharisees that a king was coming who was more powerful than David (Matthew 22:41–45; Mark 12:35–37; Luke 20:41–44). Jesus is also referred to in the third person as the One who sits at the right hand of God (Acts 2:34; Ephesians 1:20; Hebrews 1:13; 8:1; 10:12). Further, the idea of a king who is also a priest is used in Hebrews as a part of the basis for understanding Jesus' own high priesthood (Heb. 5:6; 7:17, 21).

As with Psalm 2, New Testament interpreters came to see the value of Psalm 110 in understanding Jesus' role as the Messiah. Jesus is the Son of God, he sits at the right hand of God, and he is the King who is also a Priest. It is important to note, however, that while the original context of these psalms was for political rule and the military power of the king, the New Testament authors reinterpreted Jesus' role as Messiah in terms of spiritual rule—the kingdom of God. And as the nations were the Messiah's inheritance, Jesus' new kingdom opened the way for non-Israelites, Gentiles, to be welcomed under God's reign. While the Israelite kings did not succeed in ruling over the entire world, the Messiah of the Christian faith, Jesus, has been given the power to reign over all of life. He truly is the Lord of all!

BIBLE FREEDOM

Bible freedom is an important Baptist distinctive. *Bible freedom* refers to an individual's freedom to interpret the living and active Bible under the lordship of Christ. Changing interpretations of Psalms 2 and 110 are examples of Bible freedom at work—from seeing these psalms as applied to the Davidic king, then to a future messiah, and then finally to Jesus. As the word of God is living and active, each generation who reads it can find application to their needs. As Baptists, we are grateful to have the freedom to try to continually understand Scripture and its meaning in our ever-changing contexts.

This Lesson and Life

Jesus' lordship over all includes our own individual lives. Like the nations, we are given instructions in Psalm 2:11–12 on how to live in the acknowledgement of that lordship. First, we can "serve the LORD with fear." When we serve in fear, we use our lives and the things that we do as ways of service to pay proper respect and reverence ("fear") to God. Second, we can celebrate his rule "with trembling." Celebrating Jesus' rule means not trying to take control of our own lives in opposition to him, but rather respecting Jesus' rule by submitting to God's purposes and desires. And third, we can "kiss"—honor—"the Son," Jesus, as King. Honoring Jesus as King means giving him the worship and adoration he deserves as Lord over all. Then, in that service, submission, and adoration, we will be able to seek refuge and shelter in the Son of God. When we do, we will find the blessings of living under the lordship of Christ.

QUESTIONS

1. How do we understand the violence of God and his king toward the nations in the original contexts of Psalms 2 and 110?

2. In what ways do God and Jesus function as "king"?

3. What is the difference between Christ's function as king and his function as priest in our lives?

4. In addition to the ways mentioned in these lesson comments, how can we demonstrate Christ's lordship over our lives?

NOTES ————————————————————————————————————

1. Unless otherwise indicated, all Scripture quotations in lessons 1–2, 4–13 are from the New International Version (1984 edition).

FOCAL TEXT
Psalm 8

BACKGROUND
Psalm 8

MAIN IDEA
God's majestic greatness is seen
in all of creation, including the
place he gave to human beings.

QUESTION TO EXPLORE
Where have you seen
God's greatness?

STUDY AIM
To identify how I have
recognized God's greatness

QUICK READ
Psalm 8 is a song of praise
to the God who is more
majestic than any other
being in existence, but who
still cares for and gives
honor to human beings.

LESSON TWO
God's Majestic Greatness

Psalm 8 was the first biblical text to land on the moon. Apollo 11 carried with it a silicon disc the size of a fifty-cent piece to be left on the moon. In addition to the names of astronauts, administrators, and politicians who made the landing on the moon possible, the disc also contained goodwill messages from seventy-three countries around the world. All of the names and messages were reduced 200 times so that the disc could be read only through a microscope.

One of the countries to leave a message on the disc was the Vatican. In his message, Pope Paul VI included the text of Psalm 8.[1] The psalm's proclamation of the majesty of God in his created heavens and earth and its acknowledgement of humanity's place in that creation made Psalm 8 an excellent choice for such an historic journey.

PSALM 8

For the director of music. According to *gittith*. A psalm of David.
1 O LORD, our Lord,
       how majestic is your name in all the earth!
    You have set your glory
       above the heavens.
2 From the lips of children and infants
       you have ordained praise
    because of your enemies,
       to silence the foe and the avenger.
3 When I consider your heavens,
       the work of your fingers,
    the moon and the stars,
       which you have set in place,
4 what is man that you are mindful of him,
       the son of man that you care for him?
5 You made him a little lower than the heavenly beings
       and crowned him with glory and honor.
6 You made him ruler over the works of your hands;
       you put everything under his feet:
7 all flocks and herds,
       and the beasts of the field,

> ⁸ the birds of the air,
>   and the fish of the sea,
>   all that swim the paths of the seas.
> ⁹ O LORD, our Lord,
>   how majestic is your name in all the earth!

Quotations of Psalm 8 in the New Testament

Matthew 21:16; 1 Corinthians 15:27;
Ephesians 1:22; Hebrews 2:6–8

No Greater Majesty (8:1–2)

Psalm 8 is the first song of praise in the Psalms. Psalms 1—2 function as introductory psalms. Then Psalms 3—7 are lament or petition psalms in which someone is in trouble or suffering and is calling out to God for help. As the first song of praise, Psalm 8 is also unique in that it is the only psalm that addresses God directly in the second person (you), rather than acting as a reminder to praise God or as a descriptor of reasons to praise.

Psalm 8 begins with a refrain that is repeated at the end of the psalm. While the duplication of "LORD, our Lord" might seem awkward in the English translation, the Hebrew words for Lord represented here are different. When the word *Lord* appears in small caps, it stands for the specific divine name of the God of Israel, which is sometimes pronounced *Yahweh*. However, in the Hebrew, this word was never supposed to be actually vocalized out of respect. This type of respect for the divine name is reflected in the third commandment, which is about not misusing the name of the Lord (Exodus 20:7). English translations, therefore, often translate the divine name as "LORD" to show the same respect, but use the small caps to distinguish it from the actual word for Lord, which is also included in this verse.

So the psalm begins by emphasizing that "the LORD," the specific God of Israel, is "our Lord," the One who has power and lordship over all. "How majestic is your name in all the earth!" makes a clear connection between the divine name of the God of Israel and the majestic name to be praised. A name can often function as a representation of the entire character and works of an individual. Therefore, when God's name is praised, the complete essence of God is exalted as "majestic" (or *sovereign*), which is an adjective used often in conjunction with the power and dominion of kings.

Moving from earth to the heavens, the psalmist now announced that God's glory is even above the heavens. The Hebrew word for "glory" is similar to the word for "majesty," and is also often used of the splendor of earthly kings. But for God's glory to be above the heavens emphasizes how God's majesty is far greater than any earthly king since God's reign includes both earth *and* heaven. God's majestic power is even so great that he is able to use the speech of vulnerable, powerless babies to defeat any enemies.

You Think About Me? (8:3–4)

Now the psalmist's attention turned from God to humanity. The first two verses are a celebration of the fact that no greater power exists in the universe than the one and only God of the Israelites, who is also the

---

THE HEADING OF THE PSALM

Psalm 8 is attributed to being "a psalm of David" in the heading. However, the superscriptions of the psalms were later additions to the collection and so question remains as to who the actual author of the psalm was. Indeed, it is possible that David was the author, and we could imagine a young David having many opportunities to gaze into the night sky as a shepherd.

Additionally, the superscription includes the phrase, "according to *gittith*." The *gittith* might somehow have been associated with the Philistine town of Gath. It might have been an instrument that was local to the town, a particular kind of tune or phrasing to which the psalm would have been played, or perhaps even a religious festival or occasion the town celebrated. The exact meaning of the word is uncertain.

Creator. Knowing this to be true, we can imagine the psalmist gazing into the night sky with wonder. The psalmist saw the moon and the stars and knew them to be created and set into place by the very fingers of God. In the face of such amazing majesty, the psalmist asked, "What is mankind that you are mindful of them, human beings that you care for them?" (Psalm 8:4, author's translation). The psalmist wondered how a God who is so powerful could actually think about or, even more, care for human beings.

Our point of view is different from that of the psalmist. When the psalmist looked into the night sky, scientific details about the moon and stars were not available as they are to us. When we look at the moon, we may think about earth's orbit, the solar system, and moons that orbit other planets. When we look at the stars, we may be reminded that our sun is one little star in the midst of a giant galaxy, and that galaxy is only one of possibly billions of galaxies.[2] So when we look up to the night sky, our perspective may lead us to wonder about God. Is there a God in that massive sky? Could there be a God big enough to create billions of galaxies? But rather than asking questions about God, the psalmist looked up and wondered about human life. Rather than wondering how God created the universe, the psalmist wondered how God would care for these tiny little creatures called humans. And although the psalmist wondered how and why, there was no doubt in the psalmist's mind that the God who is greater than any power in existence *does* choose to think about and care for human beings.

A Special Place of Honor and Responsibility (8:5–9)

Knowing that the great Creator considers humble human beings, the psalmist then contemplated the special place God has granted people among creation. God has made humans just "a little lower than the heavenly beings." This phrase is translated differently in various English versions. The difficulty is in translating the Hebrew word 'elohim, which is translated "the heavenly beings" in the printed Scripture text for this lesson (NIV84). This word is most commonly translated "God" (see NSRV and NASB). Although the word is plural, its plural form is thought to be used in reference to *the* God and is demonstrative of God's greatness. However, the word can also refer to multiple gods. Although there is not agreement among scholars on how to translate the word in this psalm, the translators of the New International Version (NIV84) chose to translate the phrase here to connote "heavenly beings" just as they did in Psalm 82:1 when God gives judgment among the "gods" (or "heavenly beings") in the great heavenly assembly. But no matter how the word is translated, it is clear that the psalmist intended to emphasize the unique place of humanity as being created to exist only a little lower than any beings who dwell in the heavens.

That unique place of humans also includes being crowned with glory and honor. Just as God is ascribed glory and majesty beyond that of any earthly king, so too are humans given honor. But the place of honor given to people is given by God. Humans do not have the same universal sovereignty as God; they have only the special place that God has bestowed on them.

The honor that God has given people includes making them rulers over the works of their hands and putting everything—flocks, herds, animals, birds, and fish—under their feet (Ps. 8:6–7). The psalm celebrates the dominion over nature that God gave humanity in Genesis 1:26, 28. Even though God has power over all things, God has chosen to entrust people with some of that authority. Humanity has the most elevated place among creation, for people are given power over every other created thing.

This responsibility to care for God's creation is one that must be taken seriously. In this day when we often hear about environmental issues, it is increasingly more important that we remember the ecological responsibility with which God has entrusted us. God chose to give humanity a place of special honor among creation, and we must seek to honor God's choice with our actions.

Psalm 8 then ends in verse 9 just as it begins in verse 1. After the psalmist described the place of great honor and responsibility that humans have, we are once again reminded that the name of the Lord is the most majestic in all the earth. Lest we become too proud, we must remember who is sovereign over the heavens and the earth. We cannot forget that everything given humanity, including its special place of honor and its authority over creation, is given by God. When we take our elevated status or our responsibility for granted, we also take for granted the majesty of the God who has entrusted us with our position of responsibility.

I RECOGNIZE GOD'S MAJESTY

- in the night sky as I see how God has set the universe (star, planets, galaxies, and so on) into place
- in the wonders of nature God has created
- in myself as I am created in the image of God
- in these other places and experiences: _____

_____

Even though we are only a little lower than the heavenly beings, crowned with glory, and given the responsibility of dominion over nature, we are still mere mortals. Looking up into the massive sky reminds us how truly majestic God is.

This Lesson and Life

The beauty of the night sky inspired the psalmist to recognize God's greatness, but there are many ways we can see God's majesty all around us. Like the psalmist we can look to nature for inspiration. We can see the wonder of how God fashioned each piece of creation—mountains, rainbows, flowers, thunderstorms, and so much more. But also like the psalmist, we can understand God's glory by looking toward humanity.

As humans, we are created in the image of God; we are just a little lower than the heavenly beings. So when we look inside ourselves at the amazing things we can accomplish as humans, we see a reflection of the majesty of God. But although the psalmist celebrated the special place of honor we have as humans, the psalmist also helps us understand how to remain grounded. Even though we have honor and authority, we are still lower than the One who has *all* the honor and authority. As such, we should live our lives as a reflection of God's greatness. And, as the psalm, our lives should begin and end in the acknowledgment of, "LORD, our Lord, how majestic is your name in all the earth."

QUESTIONS

1. Psalm 8 is quoted in the following New Testament passages: Matthew 21:16; 1 Corinthians 15:27; Ephesians 1:22; Hebrews 2:6–8. Read these passages and consider how the New Testament authors reinterpreted the psalm.

2. In what ways do children and infants bring praise to God as mentioned in Psalm 8:2?

3. How can we keep our perspective as human beings, who are "a little lower than the heavenly beings" (Ps. 8:5)?

4. In what ways can we take more seriously our role in having authority over creation?

NOTES

1. http://history.nasa.gov/ap11–35ann/goodwill/Apollo_11_material.pdf. Accessed 10/3/2012.

2. http://imagine.gsfc.nasa.gov/docs/ask_astro/answers/021127a.html. Accessed 10/3/2012.

FOCAL TEXT
Psalm 16

BACKGROUND
Psalm 16

MAIN IDEA
The person who trusts in the Lord can rejoice in the Lord's good provision for all of life.

QUESTION TO EXPLORE
What good things has God provided for you?

STUDY AIM
To identify why I can rejoice in God

QUICK READ
David shows us how to put our full trust in God for everything we need, listing several reasons we can rejoice in the Lord for his provision and protection.

LESSON THREE
It's a Wonderful Life

The motion picture *Annie* tells the story of a little girl living in a New York City orphanage during the Great Depression. One of the most memorable scenes in the movie is when Annie starts pondering her plight as an abandoned orphan and begins to sing a song titled, "It's the Hard-Knock Life."[1] The song names the various ways in which the lives of Annie and her fellow orphans are bad. For them it was indeed "the hard-knock life." There's no doubt about it; life can indeed be hard.

Psalm 16, though, provides lyrics of a different tone. Instead of bemoaning life's struggles and trials, David wrote a song to describe why it's a wonderful life being a servant of the Lord.[2]

PSALM 16

A Mikhtam of David.
1   Preserve me, O God, for I take refuge in You.
2   I said to the LORD, "You are my Lord;
        I have no good besides You."
3   As for the saints who are in the earth,
        They are the majestic ones in whom is all my delight.
4   The sorrows of those who have bartered for another god will
        be multiplied;
        I shall not pour out their drink offerings of blood,
        Nor will I take their names upon my lips.
5   The LORD is the portion of my inheritance and my cup;
        You support my lot.
6   The lines have fallen to me in pleasant places;
        Indeed, my heritage is beautiful to me.
7   I will bless the LORD who has counseled me;
        Indeed, my mind instructs me in the night.
8   I have set the LORD continually before me;
        Because He is at my right hand, I will not be shaken.
9   Therefore my heart is glad and my glory rejoices;
        My flesh also will dwell securely.
10 For You will not abandon my soul to Sheol;
        Nor will You allow Your Holy One to undergo decay.
11 You will make known to me the path of life;
        In Your presence is fullness of joy;
        In Your right hand there are pleasures forever.

Quotations of Psalm 16 in the New Testament

Acts 2:25–28, 31

Prayer for God's Protection (16:1–2)

The psalm begins with a prayer, "Preserve me, O God." The word used for "preserve" means *to keep watch over, to guard, and to observe*. A shepherd in that day would have been familiar with the word and the idea. A shepherd's job was to keep watch over his flock. One of the images of God in the Scriptures is that of a Great Shepherd keeping watch over his flock (Psalm 23). David was now the king or *watchman* of Israel. He offered this prayer in full confidence that the Lord was able to perform what David asked. He followed it with the statement, "for I take refuge in You."

We live in a world of surveillance and hidden cameras. It is hardly possible to go anywhere—the mall, a restaurant, or a sporting event— without the possibility of being caught on camera. While this might be a disturbing fact with our society, it is a comforting reality with God. God continually watches over us. We are under eternal surveillance. We are always being watched. We are never out of the sight or the protection of God. Psalm 139:7–8 states, "Where can I go from Your Spirit? Or where can I flee from Your presence? If I ascend to heaven, You are there; If I make my bed in Sheol, behold, You are there." We can rejoice because our heavenly Father constantly watches over us and preserves us.

In verse 2 David followed his prayer with two affirmations of faith. The first is in the statement, "You are my Lord," and the second is, "I have no good besides You." David recognized that God not only watched over him but that he belonged to God. He gave God praise for giving him everything he had.

Distinction of God's Divinity (16:3–4)

David then contrasted the righteous followers of God with those who worshiped idols. Verse 3 states, "As for the saints who are in the earth, They are the majestic ones in whom is all my delight." The distinction is made between "the saints" (or *holy ones)* and those who choose to put their trust in false gods. By using this distinction, the psalmist in verse 4 rejected two practices of pagan ritual, pouring out blood offerings to the gods and using their names in utterances of magical incantation.

Psalm 16 reflects a time when the people used pagan practices in their worship. It was not unusual to use a drink offering of wine, which was a euphemism for blood in the Old Testament sacrificial system. The priest would offer the blood of sacrificed animals as a symbol of atonement for the sins of the people. The same practice was being used in the worship of idols. In some cases blood libations were tied to human sacrifice. The blood from such sacrifices was captured in a cup or vessel and poured out on the ground by the side of the altar of sacrifice as a symbol of atonement. These sacrifices often included calling out a deity's name. In Exodus 23:13, the Israelites were prohibited from calling out the names of other gods ("Do not mention the name of other gods, nor let them be heard from your mouth."). The psalm distinguishes genuine worship of the true and living God from the worship of idols. The psalmist's loyalty to God can be seen in his refusing to take part in any portion of the idolaters' empty rituals.

As worshipers of Almighty God and followers of Christ, we must be careful that our worship is pleasing to God. We must constantly take inventory of how we worship. John 4:24 teaches us, "God is spirit, and

"A MIKHTAM OF DAVID"

Psalm 16 is referred to in the superscription as "A Mikhtam of David." The word "Mikhtam" is still debated by biblical scholars today. It appears in the headings of only Psalms 16 and 56—60. Several possible meanings have been given as interpretations of this word. Some render it as a *golden* psalm to indicate the uniqueness of this most precious psalm. This interpretation extends into the belief that this psalm was stamped or inscribed on tablets of gold. Another possible meaning can be derived by comparing the meaning of the word *psalm* with the root of the word "Mikhtam." A psalm refers to a poem with the accompanying melody, or simply a song. A "Mikhtam" represents something written. It could be that the *Mikhtams* were David's written ponderings that had not been assigned a musical element at the time of their composition. Other understandings have also been suggested.

those who worship Him must worship in spirit and truth." Our worship should be pure and free from any symbol or ritual that does not glorify God.

Acknowledgement of God's Provision and Guidance (16:5–8)

The psalm continues the theme of complete trust in God for everything by describing God as "the portion of my inheritance and my cup." The word "cup" is used as a metaphor for one's present and future state in life. David personally ascribed to God the crafting of his life, which was ultimately designed to bring utmost blessings and God's perfect will. This is further expressed in verse 5 when David said of God, "You support my lot." The word used for "support" is a word that means *to grasp* or *hold*, which suggests the idea of control. The word "lot" is used here to describe the circumstances of David's life.

In David's time the practice of casting lots was used to predict the future. The exact nature of a lot is unknown. A lot could be represented either by small stones, sticks of varying lengths, flat stones like coins, or even some sort of dice. The method of choosing lots varied as well. In many cases, stones or sticks were placed in a bag and concealed. A person would have to pull an object out of the bag and cast it on the ground. The type of stone or the length of the stick that was chosen would determine the outcome of an event as well as render a decision on what steps to take next.

God permitted the Israelites to cast lots in order to determine his will for a given situation. The casting of lots appears in connection with the division of land under Joshua (Joshua 18:6–10). Proverbs 16:33 proclaims, "The lot is cast into the lap, But its every decision is from the LORD." After the death of Judas, the apostles cast lots to determine who would replace him (Acts 1:26). Now that we have the canon of Scripture and the guidance of the Holy Spirit, we should not be dependent on such measures as casting lots. John 16:13 states, "When He, the Spirit of truth, comes, He will guide you into all the truth." God wants us to depend on the presence of the Holy Spirit, who resides in every believer in Christ, and yield to his instructions.

The idea expressed here is that God is sovereign. That is, God controls the circumstances and outcomes of each of our lives. This does not

"SHEOL"

Psalm 16:10 uses the word "Sheol" to describe the dwelling place of the soul after death. In the Old Testament, "Sheol" was considered the place where all the dead go. It was generally held that all souls descended to "Sheol" after physical death but that there was a special place in "Sheol" that was reserved for the punishment of the wicked and unrighteous souls. Later, pious Jews believed that "Sheol" was just a temporary holding place for righteous souls who would be ushered into heaven or paradise to dwell with God.

mean that everything in our lives will be perfect, just the way we like it. We still have the responsibility to be obedient to God's word, pray for guidance in our decisions, and live our lives in a manner that is pleasing to God. It simply suggests that God is purposely involved in the events of our lives to ultimately bring about his good pleasure and divine will.

That's why the psalmist exclaimed in Psalm 16:6, "The lines have fallen to me in pleasant places." In other words, when I walk in obedience to God's word, all of my steps and decisions are ordered by the Lord. We can have joy in life because we know that the circumstances of our lives are not accidental but superseded by God's providential plan. When we recognize that our lives are in the hand of God, we can enjoy peace in any situation.

David was determined to praise God, who constantly guided him and gave him counsel. He expressed his thanksgiving to God for instructing him even "in the night," the darkest points of his life (Ps. 16:7). His hope was in God, who was a steady source of stability. "Because He is at my right hand I shall not be shaken" (16:8b).

Declaration of God's Deliverance (16:9–11)

In the final section of this psalm the psalmist made a declaration of faith in the Lord who can be trusted in every situation. Notice at the beginning of verse 9 that the psalmist used the word "therefore." After making a conclusive argument in verses 1–8, the psalmist declared in verse 9, "Therefore my heart is glad, and my glory rejoices; My flesh also will dwell securely."

In verse 10, the psalmist exclaimed, "For You will not abandon my soul to Sheol; Nor will You allow Your Holy One to undergo decay." In the Old Testament, the word *Sheol* is used to describe the place where dead souls go after life. Several interpretations are given for verse 10. First is the idea of separation from God. The verb translated "abandon" in this verse can also be expressed as *to forsake*. David joyfully expressed the idea that God would not forsake him. Even when death occurred, God would not leave the psalmist's soul in *Sheol*. Second, the verse also expresses the psalmist's faith that God would never abandon him in life. David was aware that someday he would die, but he believed his death would not occur prematurely due to an immense trial he was facing at the time he wrote this psalm. Therefore, *Sheol* in this case represents a current trial from which God would swiftly deliver David so that he, being the "Holy One" of God, would not experience "decay." Lastly, there is the idea of linking the use of the word "decay" with the idea of decomposition. The Hebrew word speaks of the decay of the physical body after it is placed in the grave or tomb.

Many interpret the use of the term "Holy One" as a prophetic inference, thus referring not to David but to the resurrection of Jesus Christ, whose body did not see decay. To this end Peter quoted David's words in his sermon on the day of Pentecost in Acts 2:25–28, 31, as well as the Apostle Paul at Antioch in Acts 13:35–37. In both instances, David's words are used prophetically as referring to the death, burial, and resurrection of Jesus Christ.

David closed Psalm 16 by rejoicing in knowing that he had God's guidance ("you will make known to me the path of life," Ps. 16:11a) and the blessing of a prosperous future ("In your right hand there are pleasures forever," 16:11c). To dwell in the presence of God is the ultimate experience in life ("in Your presence is fullness of joy," 16:11b). David used the word "forever" to describe the length of dwelling in God's presence. David expressed the idea of having a covenantal relationship with God that allowed him to never be separated from God's joyful presence.

Applying This Lesson to Life

At times we become discouraged and disheartened by many of the negative events of our lives. Things happen to us over which we have no control. God does not intend for us to worry needlessly about our days here on earth but rather to rejoice in knowing that God is in control. David in this psalm helps us to refocus the lens of our lives on the blessings God has in store for those who put their trust in him.

Are you a Christian living in defeat? Start by memorizing the words of this psalm, verse 6 in particular. You will then be able to look back at the events of your life and rejoice as you identify how "the lines" of your life "have fallen . . . in pleasant places."

QUESTIONS

1. The psalmist cited the attributes of God that were most comforting to him. As you reflect on this psalm, what attributes of God are most assuring to you?

2. What insights from this psalm can you incorporate into your life to enhance your worship of God?

3. What are some teachings of Jesus concerning life after death?

4. In what ways can this psalm change or deepen your prayer life?

NOTES

1. The lyrics can be found by doing a search on Google. Accessed 10/4/12.

2. Unless otherwise indicated, all Scripture quotations in "Introducing Psalms: Songs from the Heart of Faith," lesson 3, and the Easter lesson are from the New American Standard Bible (1995 edition).

MAIN IDEA

Even when we face our darkest hour, we can find help in God.

QUESTION TO EXPLORE

Where can we find help when we face our darkest hour?

STUDY AIM

To identify resources for facing my darkest hour

QUICK READ

We can trust God to help us in every desperate situation we face because God has always helped his people to endure tough times.

LESSON FOUR
Trusting God in the Darkest Hour

The phrase *like father, like son* does not apply to my dad and me in one specific area. I scan a headline of a newspaper article, browse the first paragraph, and make an assumption about the information it contains. My father, however, reads the newspaper. I mean that he reads *the entire paper*, every word of every article. One of my boyhood memories is of Dad with paper in hand every night reading it carefully and completely.

Jesus used the first question of Psalm 22:1 as one of three things he prayed while he suffered on the cross for our sins. He said, "My God, my God, why have you forsaken me?" (Matthew 27:46). We may misunderstand what Jesus meant unless we read the entire psalm. Jesus probably followed the first-century practice of quoting the opening line of a poem in order to draw attention to the entire poem. In light of that custom, we must read this entire psalm in order to know what Jesus meant.

This psalm is a song of thanksgiving to God. Hebrew psalms of thanksgiving have two distinct parts. The first component is a complaint registered with God. The author of Psalm 22 had faced a desperate situation that he thought would take his life. In this dark night of his soul, he prayed for God's help because he trusted God (Psalm 22:1–21). The second component of a thanksgiving poem is the psalmist's response to God's answering his prayer (Ps. 22:22–31).

Psalm 22 conveys an intensity of emotion hardly found elsewhere in the Book of Psalms. The language is comprehensive in describing the despair of suffering and the declaration of thanksgiving. That may be why Jesus found this psalm so meaningful with regard to his own earthly life. Gospel writers followed the lead of Jesus. They utilized Psalm 22 in interpreting the suffering and death of Jesus. Of the thirteen Old Testament references that they used in this way, eight are from the Psalms, and five of the eight are from Psalm 22 (two from Ps. 69 and one from Ps. 31).[1]

PSALM 22

For the director of music. To the tune of "The Doe of the Morning." A psalm of David.
1 My God, my God, why have you forsaken me?
   Why are you so far from saving me,

so far from the words of my groaning?
2 O my God, I cry out by day, but you do not answer,
      by night, and am not silent.
3 Yet you are enthroned as the Holy One;
      you are the praise of Israel.
4 In you our fathers put their trust;
      they trusted and you delivered them.
5 They cried to you and were saved;
      in you they trusted and were not disappointed.
6 But I am a worm and not a man,
      scorned by men and despised by the people.
7 All who see me mock me;
      they hurl insults, shaking their heads:
8 "He trusts in the LORD;
      let the LORD rescue him.
   Let him deliver him,
      since he delights in him."
9 Yet you brought me out of the womb;
      you made me trust in you
      even at my mother's breast.
10 From birth I was cast upon you;
      from my mother's womb you have been my God.
11 Do not be far from me,
      for trouble is near
      and there is no one to help.
12 Many bulls surround me;
      strong bulls of Bashan encircle me.
13 Roaring lions tearing their prey
      open their mouths wide against me.
14 I am poured out like water,
      and all my bones are out of joint.
   My heart has turned to wax;
      it has melted away within me.
15 My strength is dried up like a potsherd,
      and my tongue sticks to the roof of my mouth;
      you lay me in the dust of death.
16 Dogs have surrounded me;

a band of evil men has encircled me,
they have pierced my hands and my feet.
[17] I can count all my bones;
people stare and gloat over me.
[18] They divide my garments among them
and cast lots for my clothing.
[19] But you, O Lord, be not far off;
O my Strength, come quickly to help me.
[20] Deliver my life from the sword,
my precious life from the power of the dogs.
[21] Rescue me from the mouth of the lions;
save me from the horns of the wild oxen.
[22] I will declare your name to my brothers;
in the congregation I will praise you.
[23] You who fear the Lord, praise him!
All you descendants of Jacob, honor him!
Revere him, all you descendants of Israel!
[24] For he has not despised or disdained
the suffering of the afflicted one;
he has not hidden his face from him
but has listened to his cry for help.
[25] From you comes the theme of my praise in the great
assembly;
before those who fear you will I fulfill my vows.
[26] The poor will eat and be satisfied;
they who seek the Lord will praise him—
may your hearts live forever!
[27] All the ends of the earth
will remember and turn to the Lord,
and all the families of the nations
will bow down before him,
[28] for dominion belongs to the Lord
and he rules over the nations.
[29] All the rich of the earth will feast and worship;
all who go down to the dust will kneel before him—
those who cannot keep themselves alive.

> ³⁰ Posterity will serve him;
>   future generations will be told about the Lord.
> ³¹ They will proclaim his righteousness
>   to a people yet unborn—
>   for he has done it.

Quotations from Psalm 22
in the New Testament

Matthew 27:43, 46; Mark 15:34; John 19:24; Hebrews 2:12

Trusting God in Our Past (22:1–11)

The author of Psalm 22 was conflicted. His theology said that God could be trusted to deliver his people if they called out to him in their distress. His experience, however, contradicted his theology. He had called out to God in his suffering, and deliverance had not occurred. He was troubled and terrified because he felt that God had abandoned him.

Two phrases in verse 1 convey his tension. The Israelites usually described God in terms of community, as *our* God. The phrase "*my* God" (italics added for emphasis) was rare and reflects the presence of an intimate relationship with God. This poet had a strong personal relationship with God. "Forsaken" is from the Hebrew verbal root *to leave*. This leaving by God placed him "far" from the psalmist (used twice in 22:1 and once in 22:11).

The psalmist consistently prayed that God would help him but received no answer (22:2). Yet he still believed in God (22:3–5). Note that the word for "trust" or "trusted" occurs three times in verses 4 and 5. He trusted God because his community of faith in the past had trusted God, and God had delivered them. Was he thinking about the liberation from slavery in Egypt or the repeated deliverance from their enemy oppressors during the period of the judges (and the kings)? God's repeated deliverance of his people in the past was the basis of the poet's theology. It was also the basis of his current tension. The God who delivered others had not delivered him in his time of need.

TITLES FOR THE PSALMS

Of the 150 psalms, 101 have titles or headings. These titles were not part of the original poems. They were added later to provide help to the Israelites in using them in worship. The title of Psalm 22 contains three statements. It is one of 73 psalms identified as "a psalm of David." These psalms are gathered in two sections of this book (Pss. 3—41 and 51—72). The traditional view is that this phrase means that David wrote these poems. Others believe that it merely designates them as being a part of the Davidic collection.

The other two statements in the title of Psalm 22 are technical musical expressions. "For the director of music" occurs in 55 of the psalms and in Habakkuk 3:19. The primary sense of this word is *to beam or shine,* and then *to lead or direct others* (as in 1 Chronicles 15:21). "The Doe of the Morning" probably refers to the melody to which the worshipers should sing the psalm.

The poet complained again to God (22:6–8) because he was the target of ridicule and hostile insults from others. They had no sympathy for him. They questioned whether he enjoyed such a close relationship with his God as he thought. If he did have such a close relationship with God, why was he hurting so much? He felt trampled or crushed by these critics and felt himself to be less than human, or wormlike (22:6).

On occasion family members have conflict with each other. During these times they may say some negative things about their loved ones, but they do not like others saying those things. This poet had questioned the absence of God, but he did not like the assertions made by others (22:8). Their attack on his faith fortified him with new strength (22:9–11).

The psalmist trusted God because God had delivered his people in the past, and he also trusted God because God had been present with him during his entire life. In essence he declared that he and God had a significant history (22:9–10). God had played a role in his being born into this world and had guided him since his infancy. The psalmist reverted to the language of verse 1 with the reference to "my God" (22:10). This memory of the presence of God painfully reminded him of the absence of God that he experienced at the moment. Consequently, he asked God to come near and help rather than stay far away (22:11). He had no one else except his God in whom he could trust.

Trusting God in Our Prayers (22:12–21)

This section of the psalm contains the most graphic description of the terrifying struggles the psalmist faced. He reserved his strongest language to detail the trouble he felt was so near (22:11). He utilized two major categories of picture language to assert how he felt.

First, he used animals to illustrate the vicious opposition and oppression of his enemies toward him. He felt helpless because they surrounded him like "strong bulls of Bashan" (22:12). Bashan was located across the Jordan River from Galilee and was noted for its vigorous livestock (see Amos 4:1). Bible writers often used the image of lions to describe power even as we do when we describe a lion as *the king of the jungle.* The psalmist felt the pain of malicious words, which tore him apart as a lion does its unfortunate prey (22:13, 21). His detractors pursued him relentlessly even as scavenger dogs took advantage of the wounded or injured (22:16, 20). As did lions and bulls, wild oxen also portrayed powerful predators (22:21).

In addition to animals, the psalmist referred to human anatomy. Utilizing various parts of the body this psalmist asserted his physical weariness and weakness resulting from his stress and distress. He possessed no physical stamina, stability, or steady courage (22:14). He seemed to be physically dehydrated and psychologically depressed (22:15).

The general description of the psalmist's condition is both good news and bad news. It is bad news because we are unable to determine the specific source of his grief. It is good news, however, in that we are better able to identify with his struggle in the great variety of the troubles we face. If we knew his specific situation, it would be easier to declare that his issue is not ours. The lack of specificity allows modern readers to apply his journey more readily to their pressing troubles.

The poet and his enemies did agree on one thing. Knowing how he felt, he believed that his death would be the inevitable outcome (22:15). His enemies believed that too and could not wait for, in effect, *the will to be read* so his belongings could be divided among them (22:18).

Even though the psalmist felt the physical and emotional effects of the attacks of his enemies and of the apparent absence of God, he continued to pray to God in faith (22:19–21). He realized that his "strength" had become as useless as a potsherd or broken piece of pottery (22:15); however, he still could trust in "my Strength," or his dependable God (22:19). He continued to trust God and prayed that God would do what he had not done yet. He still believed God *could* and possibly *would* deliver him from his trouble.

Trusting God in Our Praise (22:22–31)

One can easily detect that the mood has completely changed in verses 22–31. Something had happened. Either God had delivered the psalmist from his suffering or the psalmist had realized that God had been present with him (not absent) in the midst of his suffering. The misery and complaining of the previous verses has given way to praise. "Praise" is found four times in five verses (22:22–26).

The psalmist committed to praise God within his community of faith (22:22) and beyond that to "the ends of the earth" (22:27). He encouraged others to join him in that praise (22:23). The writer of Hebrews quoted this psalm to note that Jesus leads "the congregation" in giving praise to God (Hebrews 2:12).

The work of God is certainly the source of the psalmist's exuberant praise (Ps. 22:25). He rejoiced in the universal sovereignty of God (22:28). His God was powerful enough to enjoy dominion even over death (22:29–30).

Verse 24 may express the most important reason for the psalmist's high praise of God. He recognized the active presence of God with him when he was suffering. In fact, God was not absent or far from him. God had not hidden himself from the poet. I consider this verse to be the key to a proper understanding of this psalm.

I also believe that Jesus might have been thinking of the assurance of this verse when he quoted Psalm 22:1 from the cross. He wanted his followers to know he felt the presence of God even though it seemed God had abandoned him as he suffered. The best understanding of what Jesus meant requires reading this entire psalm (as my dad read the newspaper).

Since this psalm was so meaningful to Jesus, the Gospel writers noted several similarities in the respective experiences of the psalmist

A HELPFUL NEIGHBOR?

Your next-door neighbors are also followers of Jesus. You frequently dialogue with them about the faith that you share. Recently they have faced some difficult circumstances. Her father died suddenly from a heart attack. His position at work was eliminated as part of a downsizing decision. Her breast cancer has returned. They have been praying for weeks for God to help them in their emotional, physical, and economic struggles. Yesterday they declared that they are not sure they still believe God loves them and cares for them. How would you respond to these neighbors who are hurting?

and Jesus, especially in the suffering and death of Jesus. These similarities include the expression about being forsaken (Ps. 22:7; Matthew 27:46; Mark 15:34) and the taunting about being delivered (Ps. 22:8; Matt. 27:43). John may have had Psalm 22:15 in mind when he noted the thirstiness of Jesus (John 19:28). All of the Gospel writers alluded to the casting of lots for the clothes in Psalm 22:18 (Matt. 27:35; Mark 15:24; Luke 23:34; John 19:24).

Touching Your Life

The author of Psalm 22 trusted God in the darkest hour of his pain and suffering. God honored that trust. When Jesus entered his darkest hour of pain and suffering on the cross, Jesus too entrusted his life to God. God honored Jesus' faithfulness as well. When Jesus offered the opening verse of this psalm as a prayer to God, it was a cry of affirmation of trust in his Father and not a cry of desperation in the midst of trouble.

When we experience suffering and sorrow, we too cry out to God with questions that begin with *why*. Sometimes it seems God does not care or does not hear us. The suffering of Jesus has changed everything for we who trust in him. With Jesus as our example, we believe God is present with us in our troubled times and is at work for good in them.

We believe our strength and courage in trouble comes from the presence of God with us. Our responsibility is to hold on to God, to cling to him. We do that through prayer. We share with God our frustrations, and God indeed hears us.

QUESTIONS

1. In your opinion, what were the things that produced such misery within this psalmist?

2. The writer of the *Study Guide* suggests that verse 24 is the key verse in the best interpretation of this psalm. Do you agree or disagree? If you disagree, what other verse would be the key?

3. Which of the following two statements do you think is the more accurate? State the reasons for your thought.

   (a) God really did abandon Jesus while Jesus was on the cross.

   (b) The bearing of sin and the accompanying suffering made it seem to Jesus that God had abandoned him.

4. Recall a time in your life when your experience seemed to contradict what you believe about God. How did God deliver you in that crisis of belief?

5. Do you know an example of a Jesus follower who suffered much but did so in full trust of God during that time? What did you learn from his or her experience?

NOTES

1. Unless otherwise indicated, all Scripture quotations in lessons 1–2, 4–13 are from the New International Version (1984 edition).

FOCAL TEXT
Psalm 31

BACKGROUND
Psalm 31

MAIN IDEA

People who trust God
with their very lives will
find him faithful to care
for and redeem them.

QUESTION TO EXPLORE

Where can we go
but to the Lord?

STUDY AIM

To describe the psalmist's
trust in God and to trust
in God with all of my life

QUICK READ

We can fully commit
everything in life and death
to the Lord, for God has fully
committed himself to us.

LESSON FIVE
Committed to the Lord

51

We sometimes use the phrase *famous last words* to remind someone that what they said was quite different from what they did. Sometimes, however, the final words spoken before death do become in reality *famous last words*. For example, before he went to bed for the last time on earth, the legendary automaker Henry Ford declared, "I'll sleep well tonight." The actor Douglas Fairbanks, Sr., asserted, "I've never felt better." President Franklin Roosevelt said, "I have a terrific headache," prior to his death resulting from a massive brain hemorrhage.

Jesus made seven statements during his dying moments on the cross.[1] Three of the seven were prayers. One of these prayers was the famous last words of Jesus. Jesus chose the first line of Psalm 31:5, "Father, into your hands I commit my spirit" (Luke 23:46), for the last words that he would speak in his earthly body.

In the previous lesson we examined Psalm 22. That study helped us to understand why Jesus spoke the opening words of that psalm while on the cross. Psalm 31, like Psalm 22, must have been very meaningful to Jesus and because of that should be important to us. The interpretation of this psalm should remind us that we can commit all of life (including death) into the hands of our God because he is worthy of our trust.

Like Psalm 22, this psalm is a song of thanksgiving to God for deliverance from some kind of trouble (probably an extended physical illness). Thanksgiving songs consisted of two elements. First they contained a lament in which the poet described his undesirable condition and pleaded with God for help. The other component was one of gratitude to God for answering the call for help. The theme of this psalm is easily determined as it begins with trust in God (Psalm 31:1a), ends with trust in God (Ps. 31:19–24), and expresses throughout a strong trust in God (31:3–8, 14–15a).

To understand the meaning of the two phrases in the title to Psalm 31, see the small article "Titles for the Psalms" in lesson four on Psalm 22.

PSALM 31

For the director of music. A psalm of David.
[1] In you, O LORD, I have taken refuge;
    let me never be put to shame;
    deliver me in your righteousness.

2 Turn your ear to me,
   come quickly to my rescue;
   be my rock of refuge,
   a strong fortress to save me.
3 Since you are my rock and my fortress,
   for the sake of your name lead and guide me.
4 Free me from the trap that is set for me,
   for you are my refuge.
5 Into your hands I commit my spirit;
   redeem me, O LORD, the God of truth.
6 I hate those who cling to worthless idols;
   I trust in the LORD.
7 I will be glad and rejoice in your love,
   for you saw my affliction
   and knew the anguish of my soul.
8 You have not handed me over to the enemy
   but have set my feet in a spacious place.
9 Be merciful to me, O LORD, for I am in distress;
   my eyes grow weak with sorrow,
   my soul and my body with grief.
10 My life is consumed by anguish
   and my years by groaning;
   my strength fails because of my affliction,
   and my bones grow weak.
11 Because of all my enemies,
   I am the utter contempt of my neighbors;
   I am a dread to my friends—
   those who see me on the street flee from me.
12 I am forgotten by them as though I were dead;
   I have become like broken pottery.
13 For I hear the slander of many;
   there is terror on every side;
   they conspire against me
   and plot to take my life.
14 But I trust in you, O LORD;
   I say, "You are my God."

¹⁵ My times are in your hands;
  deliver me from my enemies
  and from those who pursue me.
¹⁶ Let your face shine on your servant;
  save me in your unfailing love.
¹⁷ Let me not be put to shame, O LORD,
  for I have cried out to you;
 but let the wicked be put to shame
  and lie silent in the grave.
¹⁸ Let their lying lips be silenced,
  for with pride and contempt
  they speak arrogantly against the righteous.
¹⁹ How great is your goodness,
  which you have stored up for those who fear you,
 which you bestow in the sight of men
  on those who take refuge in you.
²⁰ In the shelter of your presence you hide them
  from the intrigues of men;
 in your dwelling you keep them safe
  from accusing tongues.
²¹ Praise be to the LORD,
  for he showed his wonderful love to me
  when I was in a besieged city.
²² In my alarm I said,
  "I am cut off from your sight!"
 Yet you heard my cry for mercy
  when I called to you for help.
²³ Love the LORD, all his saints!
  The LORD preserves the faithful,
  but the proud he pays back in full.
²⁴ Be strong and take heart,
  all you who hope in the LORD.

Quotation from Psalm 31 in the New Testament

Luke 23:46

A Confessional Affirmation of Trust in God (31:1–8)

The testimony of this poet is clear. He trusted God completely. This full trust is conveyed through several words denoting security, safety, and stability. In God he had experienced "refuge" (31:1, 2, and 4). This is one of the dominant themes of the Book of Psalms. The word pictures a warrior returning from an exhausting battle and finding security within the walls of his own city. God was his "rock" and his "fortress" (31:2, 3). These synonyms denoted a remote rocky outcropping or a well-protected military outpost in rugged terrain. Whether away from home or at home, he knew the security and protection of God.

Often we express our thanksgiving to God for two things, for who God is and for what God has done. This poet's full confidence is based on those two things, the character of God and the action of God. The character of God is noted in the presence of three major words the Old Testament used to describe him. The Hebrew word *zedek* underlying "righteousness" (31:1) is the word used to describe one who behaved properly or rightly within a committed relationship to another. God always acts in the right way in conformity to the relationship he has with us. The righteousness of God is his willingness to live up to all of his commitments or to fulfill every promise he has made.

"Love" (31:7, 16, 21) renders another important covenant characteristic. This Hebrew word *hesed* refers to the loyalty of love within a committed relationship. This word does not refer to the passionate feelings a man and a woman may share for one another before marriage; rather, it refers to their committed or loyal love as partners in marriage. The psalmist trusted God because he knew that God was loyally committed to him.

The final characteristic of God noted here is "truth" (31:5). The root of this word is an architectural term describing a good foundation, one on which you can depend or rely. God is absolutely truthful. We can fully depend on him. The poet believed that the God of truth would sustain and vindicate those who belong to him and seek to live in truthfulness. On the basis of that belief, he asked God to spare him public shame (31:1) because he had chosen not to engage in worship of false or meaningless idolatry (31:6).

The verbs in 31:1–8 communicate what the poet believed God does do generally and could do specifically for him. "Deliver" (31:1) is an escape from physical danger or from emotional insecurity. "Save" (31:2)

WHAT DO THEY HAVE IN COMMON?

Stephen was one of the servant leaders in the New Testament church (Acts 6:1–7). He was put to death for his faithfulness to Jesus (Acts 7). Polycarp was a second-century Christian leader in Smyrna (modern Turkey). Like Stephen, he was martyred. When the flames would not burn his body, he was stabbed to death.

Martin Luther was a sixteenth-century Catholic monk whose protests initiated the major religious shift known as the Protestant Reformation. John Knox was the founder of the reform movement in Scotland (forerunner of the Presbyterian Church).

All of these men were worthy Christian leaders, but they have something more specific in common. Each of them followed the example of Jesus (and the psalmist) in their dying words. They expressed their strong trust in God as they finished their earthly journeys.

originally meant *to have room to breathe and move,* that is, to live in a "spacious place" (31:8). The poet desired the direction and guidance God offers to all (31:3). He wanted to experience the thrill of being liberated by God from his anguish. "Free" (31:4) was one of the technical terms used to describe God's liberation of the Israelites from Egyptian slavery. "Redeem" (31:5) was another freedom term from the context of family law, signifying the purchase of freedom for another.

Since God is completely trustworthy, the poet without reservation was willing to entrust his entire life to the security of God, or into God's hands (31:5). He declared that whatever happened to him was up to God in his sovereignty. The word translated "spirit" (31:5) could mean *spirit, wind,* or *breath.* It is the animating, life-giving force that God breathed into the first created human (Genesis 2:7). It refers to the totality of one's life. The affirmation of verse 5 is one of unconditional surrender of life to God.

The Continuing Affirmation of Trust in God (31:9–18)

This poet's confessed or professed trust in God provided him strength during the most difficult experiences of life. He requested mercy from

God because he was in "distress" (Ps. 31:9). This is the same word translated "anguish" in verse 7. It is a general term that may refer to sickness, sorrow, persecution, or extreme disappointment. His distress, whatever it was, had taken a toll on him. Note how he described his dramatic physical deterioration (31:9–10).

This distress also included negative reactions from both enemies and friends (31:11–13). Evidently both friend and foe mistakenly thought his trouble was God's judgment on his sinfulness. They brought false accusations against him. Their attack made him feel threatened, much as the prophet Jeremiah felt (compare 31:13 with Jeremiah 20:10).

The psalmist's enemies were arrogant and hateful, while his friends were indifferent and neglectful. He felt that his life was as useless as a piece of broken, and no longer needed, pottery (Ps. 31:12). The legendary Baptist musician B. B. McKinney was the associate pastor of Travis Avenue Baptist Church in Fort Worth, Texas, when he wrote the gospel song, "Have Faith in God." He wrote it to encourage the men during the Great Depression years who also felt discouraged and useless because they could find no work and had no ability to provide for their family.

One might think that this psalmist would give up his commitment to God because of his distress. In spite of the disturbing challenges the psalmist faced, he maintained, however, a strong trust in God (31:14). The first line of verse 15 is a paraphrase of the first line of verse 5. The line in verse 15 is not just a remark on the passing of time. The "times" (31:15) are the times of decisive moments in which a person may make good or bad decisions. Human life consists of a series of these moments.

It is appropriate for followers of Jesus to live as this psalmist did. We should live surrendering our lives to the power and guidance of God rather than seeking to control and manipulate circumstances to our own advantage. The psalmist's life was in God's hands, and he requested God to deliver him "from my enemies" (31:15). The shining of the face of God is a picturesque way of describing God's favor and blessing (31:16).

The poet believed that the righteous God would do things to set everything right for him (31:17–18). When that occurred, God would vindicate his truthfulness, while the enemies would be known as the ones who were speaking malicious and lying words.

WHERE ELSE DO WE GO?

The Question to Explore for this study is, "Where can we go but to the Lord?" The psalmist asserted that he chose not to go anywhere else, for he despised worthless idols (Ps. 31:6). In reality people can (and do) seek help and security in a variety of places other than the Lord. Some of these alternatives are as follows:

- Material possessions
- Human intellect and strength
- Human morality and goodness
- Family relationships
- Chemical substances

What other alternatives to trust in God come to your mind? What's the problem with them?

A Climactic Affirmation of Trust in God (31:19–24)

In this closing section the mood shifts from complaint to praise. The psalmist rejoiced in the presence of God, who had sustained him through his distress. He declared the goodness and protective presence of God (31:19–20). He then expressed how he himself had experienced that goodness (31:21–22). Finally, he generalized his own experience as a possibility for all and encouraged others to maintain their trust in God during difficult times (31:23–24).

The psalmist's refuge or security in God provided strength for the anguish he experienced. Note that God rescued him *in the midst of* the suffering and not *from* it. God's goodness did not come in the form of an easy life but in the form of strength in the difficult times of his life. This "stored up" goodness (31:19) was ultimately seen by all with eyes to see. The psalmist asserted that it is the presence of God with his people that keeps them secure.

God demonstrated his loyal love to this psalmist (31:21). He felt as if God was at a distance from him while he was under attack, but he discovered that God was not at a distance at all. The psalmist's suffering had not separated him from God; rather, it bonded him to God. He felt closer to God through his calling out to God for help.

The psalmist believed that his experience could be a model for others to follow. His word of encouragement to all of God's people is one of maintaining trust in God even during distress and anguish. The uncertainties of the unknown can be faced with trust when we remember that the One to whom we have committed our lives is in control. "Be strong and take heart" (31:24) is the language also seen in Joshua 1:6–9 as words of encouragement God spoke to Joshua when he faced the challenge of leading God's people into the Promised Land.

Touching Your Life

Jesus deliberately chose Psalm 31:5 as the *famous last words* of his earthly life. These words were the last ones spoken by the suffering Messiah before his physical death. I believe Jesus spoke them in the same context as the psalmist had originally written them. That context was one in which the psalmist expressed his absolute trust in God even though he experienced physical suffering and the emotional abuse of the taunts of others. That was the same circumstance of Jesus.

The final statement of Jesus in a moment of extreme distress (Luke 23:46) was a strong affirmation of trust in his Father. This trust in God was validated by Jesus' resurrection. In the cross and resurrection of Jesus, our God of truth was working to do the right thing in our behalf.

Jesus' final words before his death should be the words with which we live every day. We can face the distressing circumstances of every day of life trusting God (1 Peter 4:19). It is when we are willing to surrender our lives to God's control that we really allow God to do his work of rightness and goodness in our lives.

QUESTIONS

1. Finding "refuge" in God is a major theme in the Book of Psalms. Increase your understanding of this term through further study in Bible dictionaries and commentaries on the Psalms.

2. Recall a distressing experience in which you tried to control or manipulate things but then surrendered the entire circumstance to God. What difference did that make?

3. Jesus used the words of Psalm 31:5. Enlarge on what Jesus did by applying the entire psalm to the life of Jesus.

4. Find the words of B. B. McKinney's gospel song, "Have Faith in God," and compare the thoughts expressed by the modern poet with those of the psalmist in Psalm 31.

NOTES

1. Luke 23:34, 43; John 19:26–27; Matthew 27:46 (Mark 15:34); John 19:28, 30; Luke 23:46.

FOCAL TEXT
Psalm 32

BACKGROUND
Psalm 32

MAIN IDEA

Joy in life comes from being forgiven, which comes from accepting responsibility for one's sin and confessing it rather than from hiding it or insisting that one is perfect.

QUESTION TO EXPLORE

Why do we avoid accepting personal responsibility for wrongdoing and receiving forgiveness when the benefit of doing so is so great?

STUDY AIM

To contrast the results of hiding wrongdoing and the benefits of accepting personal responsibility for sin and confessing it

QUICK READ

We cannot experience the joy of God's forgiveness until we are willing to take responsibility for sin and then to confess that sin to God.

LESSON SIX
The Joy of Forgiveness

In teaching an Old Testament survey class at the college level some years ago, I posed the rhetorical question, "What did Adam say when God confronted him with his disobedience?" Using irony as a teaching technique, I told them that Adam agreed with God that he had done a wrong thing and deserved to be punished. He took responsibility for his own sin. Of course, then I declared that Adam had said no such thing. I was not prepared for the students' response to my comments. Many students looked confused and began to erase or mark over the notes they had just written. The lesson I learned that day was that many of the students had a limited awareness of the content of the Bible.

The reality is that Adam refused to be accountable for his behavior, of course. What about us? The tendency to refuse to be accountable for one's bad behavior is human nature. Adam expressed it when he blamed the woman, thus refusing to accept personal responsibility for his own sin.

Psalm 32 offers another way, a much better way, to deal with human sinfulness. This poem declares that accepting responsibility for sin and confessing that sin to God is the only way to receive the forgiveness God offers. It also declares that receiving God's forgiveness brings joy.

The psalmist expressed thanksgiving to God for granting forgiveness to him. He was so filled with joy that he told his story to others. His testimony flowed into instruction. That might be the meaning of the description of this psalm in the title. It is the first of thirteen psalms described as a "*maskil.*" The root of this word implies insight gained from the instruction of another. On the other hand, the word could be an evaluation of the artistic merit of the poem rather than a statement about its content.

PSALM 32

Of David. A *maskil.*
1   Blessed is he
        whose transgressions are forgiven,
        whose sins are covered.
2   Blessed is the man
        whose sin the LORD does not count against him
        and in whose spirit is no deceit.

3 When I kept silent,
  my bones wasted away
  through my groaning all day long.
4 For day and night
  your hand was heavy upon me;
my strength was sapped
  as in the heat of summer. *Selah*
5 Then I acknowledged my sin to you
  and did not cover up my iniquity.
I said, "I will confess
  my transgressions to the LORD"—
and you forgave
  the guilt of my sin. *Selah*
6 Therefore let everyone who is godly pray to you
  while you may be found;
surely when the mighty waters rise,
  they will not reach him.
7 You are my hiding place;
  you will protect me from trouble
  and surround me with songs of deliverance. *Selah*
8 I will instruct you and teach you in the way you should go;
  I will counsel you and watch over you.
9 Do not be like the horse or the mule,
  which have no understanding
but must be controlled by bit and bridle
  or they will not come to you.
10 Many are the woes of the wicked,
  but the LORD's unfailing love
  surrounds the man who trusts in him.
11 Rejoice in the LORD and be glad, you righteous;
  sing, all you who are upright in heart!

Quotations from Psalm 32 in the New Testament

Romans 4:7–8

A Firm Conclusion (32:1–2)

The poet essentially began at the end. He announced what he had come to know through his own personal journey. He asserted that he had been blessed by God. The Book of Psalms contains more beatitudes or blessedness sayings that any other book of the Bible. The great blessing of forgiveness is the basis or foundation for all of the other blessings God grants.

The beatitudes of these verses contain significant terms that the Israelites used to describe resistance to God and to declare what God does in light of our resistance or disobedience. The word underlying "transgressions" (Psalm 32:1, 5) denotes a personal, willful rebellion against a personal God. The word translated "sins" (Ps. 32:1, and twice in 32:5 as "sin") expresses the idea of missing the mark or the target of what God expected from his people. It also depicts deviating or turning away from the true path that God has marked out for us. It is the most common Hebrew word for sin in the Old Testament.

In addition, the word rendered "sin" in verse 2 ("iniquity" and "guilt" in 32:5) speaks of sin as perversion or distortion borne out of a lack of respect for God. It refers to both the act of sin and the feeling of guilt by the person who sinned. These terms suggest the full dimension of human evil that places us in a position in which we need God's forgiveness.

The poet also used three different words to describe God's forgiveness. The root meaning of "forgiven" (32:1; Hebrew *nasa*) is *to lift, carry, or take away.* When God forgives us, he takes away our sin by bearing or carrying our sin himself. The basic meaning of "covered" (32:1) is exactly that. It denotes the covering of something. The act of covering something conceals or hides that which is covered. That is probably what led to the use of this word to describe God's forgiveness. It is *out of sight, out of mind* as God hides or conceals our sins from both us and himself.

The verb in the phrase "does not count against him" (32:2) has a thinking or planning process as its basic meaning. For more information about this word, see the small article, "Credited to Us." When God forgives us, he no longer holds our sins against us. God evaluates or counts us as right although we are wrong (sinful). This restored relationship with God is not possible unless we are completely honest with God. As long as we deceitfully refuse to accept responsibility for our sins, forgiveness is not possible.

A Personal Illustration (32:3–5)

The psalmist concluded that forgiveness is a blessing from God on the basis of his own personal experience. He had known both the weariness of refusing God's forgiveness (32:3–4) and the joyfulness of receiving it (32:5).

The stubborn refusal to engage God in conversation about his sin impacted the psalmist's life physically and emotionally. He experienced the interior pain and discouragement of a mind burdened with the guilt of unconfessed sin. As a result he had no joy and energy in his life. These verses provide almost a textbook description of depression and grief growing out of the guilt that comes from the presence of sin in one's life. A happy, energetic person can easily be reduced to lazy inactivity by the weight of sin. Spiritual battles do have an affect on us physically.

We may see an echo here of the ancient belief that all physical illness was a punishment of God on sin. This ancient belief was of course challenged by both the Book of Job and the teachings of Jesus (John 9). In this psalm the physical illness resulted from the psalmist's refusal to acknowledge his sin rather than from a direct punishment of God.

The word "*Selah*" (32:4, 5, 7) is found seventy-one times in thirty-nine of the psalms and outside this book only in Habakkuk 3. We do not know for certain what the term meant. It was probably a musical notation giving instructions to the one who conducted the singing of these psalms. It might have been a signal for a clash of the cymbals or some kind of pause or interlude from the chant.

The contrast between the psalmist's concealing his sin and confessing his sin is clear. Ending his silent stubbornness changed everything. Again the writer's conclusions that he asserted in verses 1–2 were validated by his personal experience (32:5). The use of the same terms makes the connection.

The confession of sin is not a work of our goodness that produces God's forgiveness; rather, it is an agreement with God that we have sinned and stand in need of God's grace. That was the point Paul made in Romans 4:7–8 when he quoted this psalm.

The thing that changes everything is the fact that *God* chooses to forgive *us*. The pronoun "you" in "you forgave" (32:5), referring to God, has the emphasis due to its position in the sentence. This statement of

God's good work comes near the middle of this poem and is the poem's thematic center.

A Wider Application (32:6–7)

The most legitimate form of marketing a product or service is to have a spokesperson who has actually purchased the product or used the service. The best advertisement is a satisfied customer. The psalmist was a *satisfied customer.* He had experienced the joy of God's forgiveness of his sins and was more than happy to tell others how they could do the same.

"Hiding place" (32:7) translates a word that denotes the protection of a covering or shelter (also in the Hebrew of 27:5; 31:20; 91:1). In order to be confident in God's protection during troubled times, one must first build a relationship of trust and reliance on him during times of peace and security. Establishing a pattern of communication with God can then continue when turbulence occurs. God does not protect us by building strong walls that prevent trouble but by surrounding us with "songs of deliverance" (32:7).

CREDITED TO US

The Hebrew word *chashab* is found in the Old Testament some 120 times. It generally refers to the activity of thinking or the creation of new ideas through reflection. It can denote a planning process, thinking something through, or making a considered judgment or evaluation. Sometimes this word is used in the sense of an accounting term. It suggests that the act of one person could be counted or credited to another person.

In Genesis 15:6, when Abram trusted God, God "credited" it to Abram or made it count for Abram's rightness. The use of this verb in both Genesis 15:6 and Psalm 32:2 is likely what motivated Paul to use both of these passages in Romans 4:1–8. Both Old Testament texts supported the apostle's position that we are made right with God through faith and not by good deeds. God gives or "credits" his rightness to us (Gen. 15:6) and does not "count" our sins against us (Ps. 32:2) when we trust him.

This protection of God is available to all who look for him and seek to be in a personal relationship with him (32:6). The choice to seek God is an individual choice. The word "godly" is the major term that describes loyal love or devotion. God is absolutely loyal to us and desires that we also be faithful to him. The one who is loyal to God will not be threatened by circumstances that may frighten others.

A Willing Instruction (32:8–11)

The major interpretive question in these verses concerns who is the speaker in verses 8–9 (or 8–10). It could be divine speech. This would mean that God was willing to provide the necessary instruction and counsel for life to this psalmist. Others, however, feel that the psalmist was the speaker. He was willing to let his testimony expand into instruction for others.

I believe that it is the psalmist who speaks here. He was willing to teach each one who would listen and who thus might benefit from his life experience.

If the psalmist were to be a successful teacher, his students could not be like horses and mules (32:9). With such animals, the force exerted through bits and bridles is needed because they have no "understanding." This word refers to one who has a clear perception or understanding and is capable of making good moral decisions.

The wisdom teachers always spoke of two options for living one's life. One could live wisely (faithfully), or one could live foolishly. These two alternatives for life are the basis of verse 10 (see also Ps. 1). "Unfailing love" is the word for loyal love or faithful kindness. The psalmist was not ambiguous about which of these options is the best. He explicitly invited his hearers to confess their sins, be forgiven by God, and express that joyfulness in song (32:11).

Touching Your Life

This psalm provides confirming testimony of the truth expressed by the Apostle John: "If we claim to be without sin, we deceive ourselves and the truth is not in us. If we confess our sins, he is faithful and just and

COVER-UP OR COVERED?

Security guard Frank Wills discovered the break-in shortly after 1:00 A.M. on June 17, 1972. Five men were arrested, and within hours the most famous cover-up in our nation's history began. Two years later, August 8, 1974, President Richard Nixon would become the only American President to resign from office. His resignation was not forced by the crime itself but by his coordination of the massive cover-up of the crime.

Lesser-known cover-ups are equally destructive in nature. Letting God "cover" our sin is the best alternative.

will forgive us our sins and purify us from all unrighteousness" (1 John 1:8–9). We are blessed by God when we refuse to deny our sin but choose to confess our sin to God and receive his forgiveness.

Augustine (A.D. 354–430) was one of the most significant theologians in the early centuries of the Christian movement. Psalm 32 was his favorite psalm. It is said that he had this psalm inscribed on the wall above his bed so that these words would be the first ones he saw every morning when he awakened.

That is indeed a good way to start each new day. Welcoming each new gift of time from God with joy because we have been blessed with God's forgiveness is the source of the spiritual energy for living each day in faithfulness to God.

QUESTIONS

1. What key points would you make in your own testimony regarding the joy and blessing of receiving God's forgiveness?

2. The lesson comments state that the blessing of forgiveness is the foundation of all other blessings we receive from God. Do you agree or disagree with this statement? Explain your thoughts.

3. People are most like God when they forgive others. What were the circumstances when you experienced the joy resulting from someone forgiving you in the spirit of God's love?

4. Who do you think is the one speaking in verses 8–10? What are the implications of your perspective?

5. Reflect on Psalm 1 in light of Psalm 32. As a result of your
    reflection, did you conclude that the blessed one in Psalm 1 is a
    perfect person or a forgiven sinner?

FOCAL TEXT
Psalm 34

BACKGROUND
Psalm 34

MAIN IDEA
Faithfulness to God and
God's instruction is the
source of true life.

QUESTION TO EXPLORE
When we take all of
life into account, where
is true life found?

STUDY AIM
To identify the source of true
life and to affirm or reaffirm
that source for my own life

QUICK READ
When we discover that God
is the source of true life, we
should be willing to share
with others our personal
experience with God.

LESSON SEVEN
Desiring Life and Finding Its Source

My wife and I have been married for more than forty years. Prior to our wedding, we chose Psalm 34:3 as the goal of our life together. We have tried to glorify the Lord and exalt his name through serving him. In addition, I quoted this verse on the dedication page of my Ph.D. dissertation. Moreover, this is the framed verse presented to the parents when our church dedicated our two youngest granddaughters. Too, for Christmas one year, our children gave my wife a stone patio bench with this verse inscribed on it along with the names of our six grandchildren. I love this psalm.

Like some of the other psalms included in this study, Psalm 34 is an expression of thanksgiving to God for some act of deliverance coupled with the desire to instruct others in how God had blessed the poet's life. The instructional or wisdom elements can be detected in both form and content. This poem contains some of the most prominent themes of Israel's wisdom movement including the two ways to live (wise and wicked) and the fear of the Lord.

Psalm 34 is an acrostic or alphabet poem. The number of verses (twenty-two) is the number of the letters in the Hebrew alphabet. In acrostic poems, each two-line couplet or each verse begins with a successive letter of the alphabet (the Hebrew letters from *aleph* to *tau*, similar to our *A* to *Z*). Writing alphabet poems was prominent among the wisdom teachers. They used them to make a comprehensive statement about a given subject. In other words these poems covered a subject, we might say, from *A* to *Z*. The most familiar of the acrostic or alphabet poems are Proverbs 31 (the virtuous woman) and Psalm 119 (the word of God). The Book of Lamentations also contains this kind of poem. Psalms 34 and 25 are identical in the way they use the alphabet in their form.

This psalm belongs to the Davidic collection. It is one of thirteen in this book whose superscription or heading states a connection with a specific event in the life of David. The heading seemingly refers to the events recorded in 1 Samuel 21:10–15, when David acted in a bizarre way in order to be sent away by the Philistine king. For some reason, the heading identifies Abimelech as the king, while the Samuel passage calls him Achish. One possible explanation of this difference suggests that Abimelech was a generic title for Philistine kings, while Achish was a personal name.

PSALM 34

Of David. When he pretended to be insane before Abimelech, who drove him away, and he left.

1 I will extol the LORD at all times;
   his praise will always be on my lips.
2 My soul will boast in the LORD;
   let the afflicted hear and rejoice.
3 Glorify the LORD with me;
   let us exalt his name together.
4 I sought the LORD, and he answered me;
   he delivered me from all my fears.
5 Those who look to him are radiant;
   their faces are never covered with shame.
6 This poor man called, and the LORD heard him;
   he saved him out of all his troubles.
7 The angel of the LORD encamps around those who fear him,
   and he delivers them.
8 Taste and see that the LORD is good;
   blessed is the man who takes refuge in him.
9 Fear the LORD, you his saints,
   for those who fear him lack nothing.
10 The lions may grow weak and hungry,
   but those who seek the LORD lack no good thing.
11 Come, my children, listen to me;
   I will teach you the fear of the LORD.
12 Whoever of you loves life
   and desires to see many good days,
13 keep your tongue from evil
   and your lips from speaking lies.
14 Turn from evil and do good;
   seek peace and pursue it.
15 The eyes of the LORD are on the righteous
   and his ears are attentive to their cry;
16 the face of the LORD is against those who do evil,
   to cut off the memory of them from the earth.

¹⁷ The righteous cry out, and the LORD hears them;
    he delivers them from all their troubles.
¹⁸ The LORD is close to the brokenhearted
    and saves those who are crushed in spirit.
¹⁹ A righteous man may have many troubles,
    but the LORD delivers him from them all;
²⁰ he protects all his bones,
    not one of them will be broken.
²¹ Evil will slay the wicked;
    the foes of the righteous will be condemned.
²² The LORD redeems his servants;
    no one will be condemned who takes refuge in him.

Quotation from Psalm 34 in the New Testament

1 Peter 3:10–12

Glorify the Lord (34:1–3)

Many people like to brag about where they live, where they went to school, or the sports teams they follow. The psalmist began his poem by doing some high-powered bragging. He was not bragging about his own achievements or those of his national heritage, though. He asserted that he was going to brag on God and encouraged others to join him.

The verbs convey the full extent of the psalmist's pride in God. The root meaning of "extol" (34:1) is *to bow or kneel in humility before a king*. This Hebrew word *barak* is usually translated *bless*. "Boast" (32:2), the same word as the word translated "praise" in verse 1, is the word *hallal*, the basis of the first part of our English word *hallelujah*. It denoted the recognition of the nature of God that calls forth our adoration. The term "glorify" (34:3) literally means *to make great*. It describes the public declaration of the greatness of God. Finally, "exalt" (34:3) means *to raise up or elevate something*. It was used to describe the lifting of water from a well.

The psalmist was serious in his bragging about what the Lord had done for him in his life. The word "afflicted" (34:2) can also be rendered as *poor or humble*. It usually carries the sense of having been delivered from some crisis or trouble. This word is prominent in Psalms 9 and 10. The psalmist encouraged others to join him in bragging on God.

Seek the Lord (34:4–7)

In these verses the psalmist revealed that God had delivered him from a troubling situation (34:4, 6). "This poor man" (34:6) is the same word as "afflicted" in verse 2. The psalmist then used his own personal experience as a basis for declaring to others that God could deliver them as well (34:5, 7). We still draw strength from such a testimony, believing that since God has helped others, he will help us, too.

The goal of the children's game *hide and seek* is to seek to find people who are hiding and do not wish to be found. That is not the concept of the word translated "sought" in verse 4. God does not hide from us; rather, God makes himself available. *Darash*, the Hebrew word translated "sought" in this verse, is a technical term in the Old Testament for meeting God through worship. The worshiper knows where God is and goes to the sanctuary to find guidance from him or to secure a restored relationship with him through the offering of a sacrifice. This poet received his answer from God, an answer that seemingly included some kind of saving deliverance.

When we genuinely seek God, we can trust God to deliver us from trouble and to protect us. "The angel of the Lord" (34:7) is the one through whom we experience this protection. For more information about this expression of God's presence, see the small article, "The Angel of the Lord." The significance of what it means to fear God is the focus of the next section.

Fear the Lord (34:8–14)

This poet never asked others to look at him. He encouraged them to look to God. Readers should not take his word about God. They should experience God for themselves. To "taste" the Lord (34:8) is to find out by personal experience whether God is verified to be who others declare him to be. The goodness of God was one of Israel's most emphatic affirmations. The one who is willing to try God will be blessed and not disappointed.

It is hard to overestimate the importance of what it meant to "fear the LORD" (34:7, 9 [twice], 11). It did not mean that one should live in fearful terror of God. To "fear" God was *to have an extreme reverence or respect for God, to trust God completely, and to express total dependence on God.* It was another way of declaring that one realized that God is the source of life and blessing. God is worthy to trust and serve. The fear of the Lord is the starting point for the ability to live one's life wisely (Proverbs 1:7). It is the attitude in which one develops a spiritual or moral life.

The reality of fearing God or trusting him could be seen in the way one behaved in both word and deed. It involved speaking the truth instead of using the gift of speech toward evil ends (34:13). It involved doing good and pursuing peace (34:14). The link between fearing God and obeying God is clear (Deuteronomy 6:2; 10:12–13).

People willing to try out the God-fearing life are assured that they will experience the goodness and blessing and security of a relationship

THE ANGEL OF THE LORD

The Old Testament contains the phrase "the angel of the LORD" almost seventy times, mostly in the narrative books rather than in the books of the prophets and poetry. Psalm 34:7 contains one of only three occurrences of "the angel of the LORD" in the Book of Psalms (also Ps. 35:5, 6). The grammatical form of the phrase requires "the" instead of the indefinite *a* in translation. The angel of the Lord was a spirit being in human form that was closely linked to the reality of *Yahweh* himself when he appeared to Abram and Moses (see Genesis 12:7; 17:1; 18:1; Exodus 3:2).

The angel of the Lord appeared in the role of divine messenger frequently. He communicated an important message from the divine realm to God's servants. He also at times came to remind someone of God's protection in time of trouble and to provide that protection (2 Samuel 24; Isaiah 37). This motif seems to be the purpose of the angel's presence in Psalm 34:7.

with God. Even the most powerful predators of the animal world might possibly be in need, but people who feared God would never be deprived (Ps. 34:10).

Honor the Lord (34:15–22)

The closing verses of Psalm 34 declare the difference in the way God responds to those who live their lives wisely and those whose lives are filled with evil. This contrast between the two ways that the righteous and the wicked live was a common emphasis of the wisdom teachers. At first glance one might conclude that those who do good will live well, and those who do evil will experience trouble only and nothing good. The psalmist's assertions are more complex than that.

It is true that *Yahweh's* attention and care is lavished on the "righteous," or *those who are living up to God's right standards*, while he is in opposition to the acts of wicked people (34:15–16). It is also true that the end result of wickedness is God's condemnation and destruction (34:21). It is not true, however, that right-living people have a divine guarantee that they will experience no trouble whatsoever.

The righteous will go through times of trouble in which they cry out to God and receive deliverance (34:17, 19). The key question is this: What is the nature of that deliverance? These verses declare that God may deliver us from trouble in one of two ways. In some instances God provides the kind of protection that insulates us from trouble or prevents it from happening (34:20). At other times God may deliver us from trouble by granting the promise of his compassionate presence, walking with us through the trouble (34:18). The common link between these two kinds of deliverance is the attentive care and oversight of our God in our behalf. Whether we are brokenhearted or have no bones broken, God is with us.

The trouble experienced by right-living people of God is the basis for the quotation of this psalm in the New Testament. In his first letter, Peter wrote to a community of followers of Jesus who faced slander and persecution from a hostile world. He introduced his comments to address that issue by quoting Psalm 34:12–16 (1 Peter 3:10–12). He encouraged his readers to seek peace in all of their relationships with the knowledge that they still would experience trouble. They should, therefore, face this

R-E-S-P-E-C-T

"R-E-S-P-E-C-T" is not just a song title from years ago.[1] It is a desperately needed attitude in modern life.

Consider: You have a colleague at work who shows no respect for anyone or anything. He constantly criticizes his boss in derogatory terms. He uses the name of God in profane ways. He claims to have no respect for authority figures including law enforcement officers, politicians, or Christian leaders. He is completely cynical and skeptical about every cultural institution. How would you seek to encourage him to show reverence or respect for God?

circumstance with the attitude of Jesus, who himself suffered unjustly (1 Peter 4:1).

Touching Your Life

In conversation with people dealing with issues, a well-known television psychologist often asks, "How's that working for you?" I believe that anyone who is a serious follower of Jesus could say that following Jesus works for him or her really well. When we discover that God is the source of true life and trust him with our lives, we experience God's grace-filled blessings. As a result we should desire to share that blessedness with others by bragging on God to everyone who will listen.

Authentic bragging on God will include testifying how God delivers us from trouble by protecting us and by providing for us when we experience any kind of crisis. Brag on what God has done in your life. God can use it to communicate to others the encouragement that he can do it for them as well.

QUESTIONS

1. Assume the role of an ancient wisdom teacher. Write an alphabet poem on the love of God. What elements would you include?

2. What are five things about the life and work of Jesus that would be at the top of your bragging list about him?

3. What is the evidence that God really wants to be found by those who seek him rather than to make it difficult for us to find him?

4. How do you think that church leaders could help people express more reverence and respect for God in their lives?

5. The writer of the lesson comments declared that God delivers his people from trouble in one of two ways. See under the heading "Honor the Lord (34:15–22)." Do you agree that both of these ways are deliverance? Why or why not?

N O T E S ───

1. Original lyrics by Otis Redding, with revision associated with Aretha Franklin.

MAIN IDEA
Genuine gratitude for God's
help is expressed by delighting
in doing God's will in one's life.

QUESTION TO EXPLORE
How are we to say
thank you to God?

STUDY AIM
To summarize what the psalm
teaches about how truly to give
thanks to God and to evaluate
how I am giving thanks to God

QUICK READ
The psalmist began by
expressing thanks for God's
blessings before stating a
commitment to serve God
and concluding with an
affirmation of confidence in
future deliverance from God.

LESSON EIGHT
Gratitude for God's Help

81

Life is not always easy or pretty. Often we can find ourselves struggling against our circumstances. At other times we may be struck down by unexpected news. Many times in life the waters that had been smooth yesterday are rough today. At these times it can be difficult to feel grateful or express gratitude to God for his blessings as our attention turns to finding a way out of the difficulties. We know that God is still there and still loves us, but all we can focus on is getting relief.

The Bible is full of stories of people who found themselves in similar situations. The Book of Psalms in particular is full of prayers that were cried out to God from the depths of despair. Psalm 40 is one of those psalms, and it is attributed to David. While it is unclear at what point in his life David composed this psalm, it is clear that it was a time when he felt threatened. This psalm teaches us that when life is difficult and it is hard to feel grateful, the best way to express our gratitude to God is through continuing to serve him. As we do, our problems seem to diminish as our attention is taken off ourselves and we find renewed confidence to face the future.

PSALM 40

For the director of music. Of David. A psalm.
1   I waited patiently for the LORD;
        he turned to me and heard my cry.
2   He lifted me out of the slimy pit,
        out of the mud and mire;
    he set my feet on a rock
        and gave me a firm place to stand.
3   He put a new song in my mouth,
        a hymn of praise to our God.
    Many will see and fear
        and put their trust in the LORD.
4   Blessed is the man
        who makes the LORD his trust,
    who does not look to the proud,
        to those who turn aside to false gods.
5   Many, O LORD my God,
        are the wonders you have done.

The things you planned for us
  no one can recount to you;
were I to speak and tell of them,
  they would be too many to declare.
6 Sacrifice and offering you did not desire,
  but my ears you have pierced;
burnt offerings and sin offerings
  you did not require.
7 Then I said, "Here I am, I have come—
  it is written about me in the scroll.
8 I desire to do your will, O my God;
  your law is within my heart."
9 I proclaim righteousness in the great assembly;
  I do not seal my lips,
  as you know, O LORD.
10 I do not hide your righteousness in my heart;
  I speak of your faithfulness and salvation.
I do not conceal your love and your truth
  from the great assembly.
11 Do not withhold your mercy from me, O LORD;
  may your love and your truth always protect me.
12 For troubles without number surround me;
  my sins have overtaken me, and I cannot see.
They are more than the hairs of my head,
  and my heart fails within me.
13 Be pleased, O LORD, to save me;
  O LORD, come quickly to help me.
14 May all who seek to take my life
  be put to shame and confusion;
may all who desire my ruin
  be turned back in disgrace.
15 May those who say to me, "Aha! Aha!"
  be appalled at their own shame.
16 But may all who seek you
  rejoice and be glad in you;
may those who love your salvation always say,
  "The LORD be exalted!"

> ¹⁷ Yet I am poor and needy;
>   may the Lord think of me.
> You are my help and my deliverer;
>   O my God, do not delay.

Quotation from Psalm 40 in the New Testament

Hebrews 10:5–7

Gratitude for God's Blessings (40:1–5)

David's life had truly been blessed by God. Not only had God raised him from a shepherd to become king, but God had also rescued him many times from the schemes of Saul and had given him numerous victories over Israel's enemies. As David looked back over his life, he recognized God's blessings and began this psalm expressing his gratitude for them. Verse 1 states that while David often had to wait on God's timing, God always answered. This verse contains a powerful image of the Almighty inclining or kneeling as a Father to hear the cries of his child. (The Hebrew word translated "turned" in the printed Scripture from NIV84 means *inclined*.)[1] Of all the multitude of blessings God gives us, perhaps none is greater or more meaningful in the moment than God's immediate presence in those dark nights as he kneels beside us to hear our cries and calm our hearts.

Not only did God kneel to listen to David's cry, God also reached out and lifted him out of the depths of his despair (Ps. 40:2). Often the circumstances of our lives can seem to cast us into such a dark pit that we may begin to wonder whether even God can reach us. David likely felt this level of despair when he was forced to flee Jerusalem as his son Absalom led an army against him (2 Samuel 15). Yet, David proclaimed that God went beyond lifting him from the mire. God planted his feet on secure rock (Ps. 40:2). Such a turn of fortune was a new experience for David and led him to break out in a new song of gratitude and praise (40:3). God is constantly providing us with opportunities to sing new songs of thanksgiving as he showers us with blessings that are new every day (Lamentations 3:22–23). Yet in our world where we have a scientific explanation for almost everything and where we are often busy running from one thing to another, we often miss many of God's daily miracles.

Verse 4 sounds as if it could have been written yesterday. Our world is certainly full of the proud—those who put their trust in their possessions, position, or knowledge and see reliance on God as weakness. David proclaimed that it is only the one who acknowledges and submits to God who is blessed because only such a person understands that the source of the wondrous deeds we see around us is a loving God. This awareness compelled David to proclaim his deep gratitude to God and to encourage others to do the same.

Commitment to Serve God (40:6–10)

David's gratitude could not stop with a verbal expression of thanks. He understood that God is most pleased when he sees his followers obeying his call to be representatives of God's presence in the world. For many in David's time, that meant faithfully performing all of the religious rituals prescribed in the *Torah*, the Law. This primarily consisted of bringing proper sacrifices and offerings to the temple. (Detailed descriptions of these sacrifices are found in Leviticus 1—5.) Yet in verse 6, David stated that God did not desire or require such rituals.

How should the reader understand David's words here? Scriptures such as 1 Samuel 15:22–23; Psalm 51:16–17; and Micah 6:6–8 seem to indicate that the people had come to put their confidence in the act of bringing the sacrifice. They felt that if they simply performed the right ritual in the right way, they would be clean before God. But God had not given them the rituals to be an end in themselves but to be an outward demonstration or symbol of an internal change of heart. Performing the ritual was not a cover or license to live however one wanted. It was an inner sacrifice of self and commitment to obey God in serving others that made one clean before God.

David was not here condemning the rituals of the *Torah*. Indeed the rest of the psalm and the story of his life shows that he continued to participate in corporate worship. He simply wanted to make it clear that offering sacrifices was insufficient if not accompanied by a life that internalized the heart of the Law.

HEBREWS 10:5–7

Centuries after Psalm 40 was written, the writer of the New Testament Book of Hebrews quoted Psalm 40:6–8 in interpreting Christ's sacrifice. In the context of Hebrews 10, Hebrews 10:5–7 presents Christ as declaring all previous sacrifices as being unable to deal with human sin and stating that he had come to satisfy God's requirement for forgiveness. The change in the phrase "my ears you have pierced" (Ps. 40:6) to "a body you prepared for me" (Heb. 10:5) resulted from the author's use of the Septuagint, the first Greek translation of the Old Testament. While it is unclear why the Septuagint translators altered this phrase, it fits well with the message of the writer of Hebrews. Jesus is pictured in Hebrews 10:6 acknowledging that God had prepared a physical body for him, which would be needed in order to fulfill the role of the final sacrifice.

Many have seen verse 7 as referring almost exclusively to the Messiah. This understanding may have been a factor that led the author of Hebrews to use this passage in describing Jesus as the final sacrifice (Hebrews 10:5–7; see small article titled "Hebrews 10:5–7."). In the immediate context of this psalm, though, David might have been referring to himself. The question is, to what "scroll" was he referring? Consider two possibilities. First, verses such as Exodus 32:32–33 indicate that the ancient Israelites believed that God had a book in which were the names of his people. Second, and more likely, David may have been referring to the promise that God made to Abraham that his descendants would include kings (Gen. 17:6). This promise was recorded in the *Torah*. David was thus declaring that God had again kept his promise. Because of God's faithfulness in keeping his promise, verse 8 states that David's desire, as an expression of gratitude, was to do God's will.

In verses 9–10, David stated that he had not kept to himself the news of God's actions or of his own gratitude. He had spread the word to everyone who would listen throughout the entire community. He had not held anything back. He had not claimed responsibility for any of God's actions.

How often are we guilty of doing what David here refused to do? How often do we attribute God's actions on our behalf to our own actions or to some other means? God desires to hear our gratitude and praise, but God is most fully glorified when we go beyond that to sharing such thoughts with others.

Confidence in God's Deliverance (40:11–17)

David had expressed his gratitude to God for all the blessings of the past and had committed himself to demonstrate his thanks through serving God and telling others about God. Now David proclaimed his confidence that God would once again deliver him from his current situation. His remembrance of the past acts of God and his focus on others instead of himself formed a solid basis for calling for God to deliver him and having confidence that God would indeed do that. While these verses are certainly a call for God to act, this call was uttered by one who had learned to depend on God instead of on his own abilities and who cried out in confidence that God would hear and act. Verse 11 expresses this confidence.

In verse 12 David made a confession that demonstrated an awareness that his present problems were at least somewhat due to his own previous sins. This confession may support the idea that this psalm was composed during the time of his son Absalom's rebellion (2 Samuel 15—18). In his confrontation with David following David's sin with Bathsheba in 2 Samuel 12, the prophet Nathan had informed David that he would always have trouble within his household. It can be difficult to accept that although God does forgive our sins when we confess them, we may still have to deal with the adverse consequences of our actions. Accepting that responsibility is part of learning to depend more fully on God.

In verses 13–15, the reader gets the impression that David's enemies were closing in on him. David cried out to God that God might move swiftly in coming to his aid. His main desire was not that God would exalt David over his enemies, but that God might put his enemies to shame and turn them back. David was not concerned with getting credit for the victory but rather wished that God would be shown to be the Protector of those who depend on him.

Verses 16–17 are a great statement of all that David had learned about God and about himself. He had learned that he was indeed weak and

---

PSALM 70

Many have noticed that Psalm 70 appears to be a quotation of Psalm 40:13–17. While a number of explanations have been suggested, it seems likely that Psalm 70 is an abbreviation of Psalm 40 that has been adapted for a later period and purpose. The superscription of Psalm 70 associates it with the memorial offering, and thus omitting in Psalm 70 the reference in Psalm 40:6 to sacrifices not being required would be understandable. The omission of phrases in Psalm 40 that may have called to mind the monarchy may indicate that Psalm 70 dates from the time of the Exile (sixth century B.C.) or later.

---

poor without the blessings and protection of God. He had also learned his need not only to express his thanks to God but also to show his gratitude by proclaiming God's greatness and encouraging others to do the same.

Implications for Today

The God to whom David cried is the same God to whom we pray today. We face many troubling circumstances from which God faithfully delivers us. We enjoy innumerable blessings from God's hands each day. While often we may express thanks privately or among our Christian friends, we can be tempted to keep quiet or to take credit ourselves. Psalm 40 clearly teaches us that we should not only express our gratitude to God, but also that our gratitude is most fully expressed and demonstrated when we commit to submit our will to God and boldly share the truth of God's faithfulness and mercy with others.

QUESTIONS

1. How does your life express gratitude to God?

2. When was the last time you cried out to God for deliverance?
    What happened?

3. How often do you talk about the blessings of God with those
    outside the church?

4. In what specific ways can you express thanks to God through
    your actions?

NOTES ————————————————————————————————

1. See Psalm 40:1, NASB.

FOCAL TEXT
Psalm 53

BACKGROUND
Psalms 14; 53

MAIN IDEA
Refusing to seek and follow
God results in God's judgment.

QUESTION TO EXPLORE
Since no one attains God's
standard of goodness, why
are people often so prideful?

STUDY AIM
To describe ways in which
people live as if God does
not matter and state why
doing so is foolish

QUICK READ
The psalmist described
those who wished to live in
a world without God and
oppose God's people and
then announced both God's
judgment on the foolish and
God's deliverance of his people.

LESSON NINE
No One Does Good

Over the past few years several authors known as *new atheists* have become known due to their many books and television appearances. These *new atheists*—the most widely recognized of which likely are Richard Dawkins, Christopher Hitchens, and Sam Harris—have argued that since science has now provided humanity with objective answers to the mysteries of the universe, there is no longer any need for superstitious reliance on the supernatural.

These ideas are certainly not new. While we may view these opponents of faith with concern, the reality is that many times even believers can live their lives as *functional atheists*. How? By giving little or no thought to or acknowledgment of God Monday through Saturday. They are not explicitly denying God's existence as true atheists do, but they are implicitly and practically denying God's presence and relevance in their daily lives by failing to seek God consistently in all of life.

People have been trying to ignore or deny God a place in the world since the beginning. In Psalm 53, the psalmist addressed those who would hold such attitudes and warned them that their way of life had consequences. God will judge those who refuse to acknowledge him. This psalm has much to say not only to those who deny God's existence but also to those who do not intentionally serve God in their lives.

PSALM 53

For the director of music. According to *mahalath*. A *maskil* of David.

¹ The fool says in his heart,
    "There is no God."
They are corrupt, and their ways are vile;
    there is no one who does good.
² God looks down from heaven
    on the sons of men
to see if there are any who understand,
    any who seek God.
³ Everyone has turned away,
    they have together become corrupt;
there is no one who does good,
    not even one.

> 4 Will the evildoers never learn—
>   those who devour my people as men eat bread
>   and who do not call on God?
> 5 There they were, overwhelmed with dread,
>   where there was nothing to dread.
> God scattered the bones of those who attacked you;
>   you put them to shame, for God despised them.
> 6 Oh, that salvation for Israel would come out of Zion!
>   When God restores the fortunes of his people,
>   let Jacob rejoice and Israel be glad!

Quotation from Psalm 53 in the New Testament

Romans 3:10–12

Description of the Foolish (53:1–4)

This psalm begins with one of the most well-known verses in the Book of Psalms. While the word "fool" is the best translation of the Hebrew term *nabal*, we should not associate our modern connotation of mental or intellectual deficiency with the biblical idea of a fool. In biblical terms, a "fool" was one who lacked moral or spiritual sensitivity. A "fool" was a wicked person who lived life being led by natural appetites.

In 1 Samuel 25 David encountered a man who refused to assist David and his army. The man's name was Nabal. His wife Abigail said of him, "He is just like his name" (1 Samuel 25:25). (Nabal is from the Hebrew word for *fool*.) The story shows this man clearly to have been a fool. Thus we should understand that when Psalm 53:1 states, "The fool says in his heart, 'There is no God,'" no one in the ancient world would have entertained the idea that this statement referred to an absolute absence of a deity. The ancient world was full of gods and goddesses. Yet except for the God of Israel, none of the pagan deities placed any moral expectation on humanity. As long as people performed the proper rituals in the prescribed way, the pagan gods were usually happy and did not interfere in human activity. It was thus specifically *Elohim*, the God of Israel, that the fool denied.

The fool described here was thus not a philosophical atheist like many modern atheists. Instead, this fool was a practical atheist. Such fools were not concerned with theoretical questions of God's existence. Indeed, most of them would readily concede that God exists. They sought simply to deny God a place in their lives and to act as if God did not exist. Such people did so because they inherently knew that if God did exist, they would be held accountable for the way they lived. They denied and refused to acknowledge God so they could continue to live as they chose without guilt or fear of judgment. One does not have to look hard to find many people today living with this same mindset.

Psalm 53:2 pictures God as eagerly searching the hearts of all of humanity, seeking anyone who would acknowledge him. The Hebrew term that is usually translated "understand" may also be translated *is wise.* The psalmist was thus setting up a contrast between the *foolish* and the *wise.* This contrast is used often in the Old Testament, especially in the Book of Proverbs. The foolish person is spiritually and morally insensitive, but the wise person understands that God has built into creation a moral order. The wise also understand that the God who created the universe desires a relationship with his creation. This God invites humanity, who are created in God's image to be his children, to seek to know him. The wise are those who gladly accept this invitation and actively seek God. Like the writer of Ecclesiastes, they have perhaps tried the ways of the foolish and found them empty. Now they have set their minds to follow the ways of God. These are the ones God hopes to find as he searches the earth.

Yet God's search is ultimately disappointing as he finds that all have fallen away from seeking after God. In verses 3–4, the psalmist piled up negative descriptions of what God sees as he examines the hearts of humanity. First, all have "turned away" and "become corrupt." Second, God finds "no one who does good." Third, God finds a lack of knowledge in the human heart. Fourth, God's search reveals evil people who casually destroy God's people. Finally, no one calls on the Lord for direction. The picture is of people who have deliberately turned away from God. As a result, these individuals have lost all knowledge of the truth about God and have become morally corrupt. They then fail or refuse to

---

PSALM 14

Psalms 53 and 14 are nearly identical. Apart from a few insignificant differences, the two psalms are seen to differ most clearly when comparing Psalm 14:5–6 and Psalm 53:5. Psalm 14:5–6 reads, "There they are, overwhelmed with dread, for God is present in the company of the righteous. You evildoers frustrate the plans of the poor, but the LORD is their refuge," while Psalm 53:5 states, "There they were, overwhelmed with dread, where there was nothing to dread. God scattered the bones of those who attacked you; you put them to shame, for God despised them."

Among many suggested explanations for this difference, perhaps Psalm 14 is directed specifically to individuals within the Israelite community who oppressed the poor, while Psalm 53 seems to refer to Israel's enemies who attacked them. Perhaps the composer of Psalm 53 simply took an earlier psalm and modified it to apply to a celebration of a military victory by the Israelites.

Whatever the reason for the change, taking the two psalms together shows that the foolish behavior of denying God can be carried out by those both inside and outside the community of God's people. God will judge both.

---

call out to God, and they turn against anyone who seeks to follow God. Such is clearly a picture not only of the *new atheists* but also of anyone who, for whatever reason, has turned away from fellowship with God.

God's Judgment on the Foolish (53:5)

The psalmist continued by stating that while God may be absent within one's heart, God is certainly still present and will hold the foolish accountable for their choices. The psalmist describes two ways God accomplishes his judgment on the foolish.

First, since the foolish have rejected God, God withdraws his presence from them. This leads to a situation in which the foolish sense great terror all around even though there is no terror. One of the greatest blessings we receive from being in fellowship with God is an internal

ROMANS 3:10–12

In Romans 3:10–12, Paul provided an extension of the idea in Psalm 53 that is appropriate for believers today. While it is easy for us to see others as foolish, Paul made it clear that all people are fools apart from God's wisdom. Apart from God, people lack love and righteousness, and thus all their attempts to be justified before God fail.

Paul specifically used Psalm 53 to state that the Jews, who knew the Law, were no better than the Gentiles, who did not. Mere knowledge of God and what God expects does not make one right before God because of the corruption of the human heart. Only God's righteousness allows anyone to stand before God.

peace even in the midst of chaos. Even when we walk through the dark valleys of life, we can do so without fear if we know that God is with us. But when that assurance is lacking, even the slightest bump in the night can instill great fear.

The second way God carries out judgment is more direct. The psalmist states that God puts the foolish to shame and scatters their bones. There was a clear understanding in ancient Israel that God would occasionally punish those who rejected or rebelled against Him in a physical way with either illness or death. While we should always be extremely cautious in seeing any specific tragedy or disaster as God's direct judgment, we should accept that the Creator may use elements of creation in both blessing and judging humanity. Thus whether God acts directly in punishing or simply withdraws his presence, the foolish decision to deny God or live as if God is not here leads to the consequences of God's judgment.

God's Deliverance of His People (53:6)

God's judgment on the foolish was certain, and so was his deliverance of those who were still God's people or those with the wisdom to seek

God for direction. In the Hebrew, verse 6 begins with a question, *Who will bring salvation for Israel from Zion?* As the psalmist considered how God's people were surrounded by foolish people who had rejected God and who sought to destroy God's people, he cried out for deliverance.

Yet although he phrased this cry as a question, he was certain of the answer. God would bring salvation and deliverance to his people. It is clear that God was the one who would bring deliverance since it would come from "Zion." "Zion" was seen as the earthly representation of God's presence in the midst of his people. All those who humbled themselves, acknowledged their dependence on God, and cried out for help from Zion would receive salvation.

When this salvation arrived, the only response was to rejoice. The psalmist emphasized the depth of thankfulness and rejoicing by referring to the people as both "Jacob" and "Israel." Joy would overflow when the people of God saw the salvation that came from rejecting the way of the foolish and seeking after God.

Implications for Today

There is a sad irony in our postmodern world. For all of our great technological and scientific advances, the twentieth century was characterized by constant war, violence, economic disparity, poverty, and hunger. It seems that the twenty-first century will be no better. As we have become able to explain great mysteries of how the cosmos works and have built machines to make life easy and comfortable for those who can afford them, we have decided that we do not need God. As a result, we have lost our base of morality, and truth has become whatever works for me in this moment. In the words of Psalm 53, we have become foolish.

We find a form of this in the church also as many people want only enough of Jesus to get them to heaven after they die but not enough to alter their daily life. They enjoy reading the promises of blessing God makes but skip over the call to love their enemies and become a servant to all. They gather to sing of God's grace on Sunday and yet never mention God's blessings during the week. Such individuals have lost their spiritual sensitivity. The Bible calls such a person a "fool" and declares that such a person will not escape God's judgment.

QUESTIONS

1. How do we sometimes act as practical atheists despite our faith?

2. How would you respond to someone who denies the existence of God?

3. How can we maintain our spiritual sensitivity Monday through Saturday?

4. As God searches your heart, what does he see?

FOCAL TEXT
Psalm 69

BACKGROUND
Psalm 69

MAIN IDEA
In deep distress, the psalmist in desperation cried out to God for help.

QUESTION TO EXPLORE
Where can we turn when there's no place to turn?

STUDY AIM
To summarize the psalmist's prayer of desperation and identify ways it touches my life

QUICK READ
The psalmist described his desperate situation before pleading to God for help and for justice against his oppressors. The psalm concludes with a confident expression of praise to God.

LESSON TEN
A Desperate Cry

No one's life is lived without at least a few complaints. That statement applies even to people who may be the type of personality that never verbally expresses them. These usually arise when, no matter how hard we try, life simply does not go according to our plan. Maybe it is a difficult co-worker or unexpected news from a doctor that disrupts life and focuses our attention and efforts on trying to overcome our circumstances. Such times can be especially difficult when the problems seem to be related specifically to our attempts to follow God's direction. Negative thoughts and feelings can build up as we feel we have nowhere to turn for help.

Psalm 69 was clearly written by an individual in crisis. Internal depression and outward oppression threatened to overwhelm his life. He was surrounded by people who hated him without cause and were seeking his life. To make matters worse, the threats seemed to be related directly to the psalmist's zeal in seeking to follow God's purposes for his life.

In the midst of such pressure and rejection by people and silence from God, it seemed there was nowhere the psalmist could turn for help. Yet trusting in the God he knew was there even when he did not see or hear God, the psalmist poured out his heart to God and pleaded for divine assistance. As we read this emotional psalm, perhaps we can gain a new perspective that will help us during our times of darkness.

PSALM 69

For the director of music. To the tune of "Lilies." Of David.
1 Save me, O God,
        for the waters have come up to my neck.
2 I sink in the miry depths,
        where there is no foothold.
   I have come into the deep waters;
        the floods engulf me.
3 I am worn out calling for help;
        my throat is parched.
   My eyes fail,
        looking for my God.
4 Those who hate me without reason
        outnumber the hairs of my head;

many are my enemies without cause,
    those who seek to destroy me.
I am forced to restore
    what I did not steal.
5 You know my folly, O God;
    my guilt is not hidden from you.
6 May those who hope in you
    not be disgraced because of me,
    O Lord, the LORD Almighty;
may those who seek you
    not be put to shame because of me,
    O God of Israel.
7 For I endure scorn for your sake,
    and shame covers my face.
8 I am a stranger to my brothers,
    an alien to my own mother's sons;
9 for zeal for your house consumes me,
    and the insults of those who insult you fall on me.
10 When I weep and fast,
    I must endure scorn;
11 when I put on sackcloth,
    people make sport of me.
12 Those who sit at the gate mock me,
    and I am the song of the drunkards.
13 But I pray to you, O LORD,
    in the time of your favor;
in your great love, O God,
    answer me with your sure salvation.
14 Rescue me from the mire,
    do not let me sink;
deliver me from those who hate me,
    from the deep waters.
15 Do not let the floodwaters engulf me
    or the depths swallow me up
    or the pit close its mouth over me.
16 Answer me, O LORD, out of the goodness of your love;
    in your great mercy turn to me.

[17] Do not hide your face from your servant;
   answer me quickly, for I am in trouble.
[18] Come near and rescue me;
   redeem me because of my foes.
[19] You know how I am scorned, disgraced and shamed;
   all my enemies are before you.
[20] Scorn has broken my heart
   and has left me helpless;
 I looked for sympathy, but there was none,
   for comforters, but I found none.
[21] They put gall in my food
   and gave me vinegar for my thirst.
[22] May the table set before them become a snare;
   may it become retribution and a trap.
[23] May their eyes be darkened so they cannot see,
   and their backs be bent forever.
[24] Pour out your wrath on them;
   let your fierce anger overtake them.
[25] May their place be deserted;
   let there be no one to dwell in their tents.
[26] For they persecute those you wound
   and talk about the pain of those you hurt.
[27] Charge them with crime upon crime;
   do not let them share in your salvation.
[28] May they be blotted out of the book of life
   and not be listed with the righteous.
[29] I am in pain and distress;
   may your salvation, O God, protect me.
[30] I will praise God's name in song
   and glorify him with thanksgiving.
[31] This will please the LORD more than an ox,
   more than a bull with its horns and hoofs.
[32] The poor will see and be glad—
   you who seek God, may your hearts live!
[33] The LORD hears the needy
   and does not despise his captive people.

> ³⁴ Let heaven and earth praise him,
>   the seas and all that move in them,
> ³⁵ for God will save Zion
>   and rebuild the cities of Judah.
>   Then people will settle there and possess it;
> ³⁶   the children of his servants will inherit it,
>   and those who love his name will dwell there.

Quotations of Psalm 69 in the New Testament

John 2:17; 15:25; Acts 1:20; Romans 11:9–10; 15:3

Statement of Complaint (69:1–12)

The psalmist painted a vivid picture of the circumstances that threatened to overwhelm him. He pictured the many troubles as raging flood waters that had swept into his life. Not only were the waters rising, but his feet could not find a solid place to stand, and he began to sink into the mire. In verse 1, the term that is often translated "neck" is the Hebrew term *nephesh*, which is better translated as *soul or life force*. The *nephesh* was what gave life. Thus these troubles not only threatened to overwhelm the psalmist emotionally but were also a threat to his life itself. In response to these rising flood waters, the psalmist had cried out to God until his strength was gone and his throat was parched. He was weary of waiting for God to answer and had almost given up.

Despite his weariness, the psalmist once again laid out his complaints before God. Verse 4 refers to a multitude of people who had brought charges against the psalmist. Among these charges was an accusation of theft. According to the law, he must return what he stole. While specific details were lacking, the value of the stolen goods must have been considerable as this charge dominated their case against him. If this psalm was indeed composed by David, it may be that these opponents were accusing him of stealing the throne from Saul's family. While David and his family knew that God had selected him to be king, many citizens of

PSALM 69 IN THE NEW TESTAMENT

Although Psalm 69 was originally a highly personal prayer between the psalmist and God, several New Testament writers interpreted phrases and images from this psalm as prophetic statements concerning Jesus. For example, John saw the reference to those who hated the psalmist without cause in Psalm 69:4 as directly prophetic of Jesus (John 15:25) and saw a reference to Jesus' zeal for doing God's will in Psalm 69:9 (John 2:17). Paul saw the reproaches of God falling on the psalmist in Psalm 69:9 as also demonstrated in the life of Jesus (Romans 15:3). Paul applied Psalm 69:22–23 to the gospel being proclaimed to the Gentiles (Rom. 11:9–10). Finally, Acts 1:20 applies Psalm 69:25 to Judas.

In each of these cases, a New Testament writer has interpreted an Old Testament text as being prophetic based on parallels between the psalm and Jesus. Yet the fact that New Testament authors did so does not give us license to do so ourselves. Indeed, great care should be taken when seeking to interpret an Old Testament text as prophecy.

Israel likely saw him as a usurper. This would help explain why Absalom could raise a large army to fight against David in 2 Samuel 15. This would seem to fit with the psalmist's claim that this opposition came against him as he sought to fulfill God's direction (Psalm 69:7).

In verses 5–6, the psalmist stated that he knew he had not lived a blameless life and he expressed a desire that his past mistakes might not be a reason that others who sought God would stumble and fall away. If David is the author, these verses may express a desire that he always directly lead others in the true path to God, or a desire that his life might be an example for others to follow. Yet whatever David's past weaknesses might have been, verses 7–12 make it clear that he saw his current oppression as a result of seeking to follow God. His zeal for God had caused him to be a target for ridicule by everyone, including the leaders within the community. Such an experience can apply today. The more earnestly we seek to follow God, the more we are living contrary to the world and the more the world will seek to oppose us.

Plea for God's Help (69:13–21)

Beginning in verse 13, the psalmist appealed to God once again for help. As verse 5 indicates, this was clearly not the first time he had pleaded with God. Yet despite God's apparent silence and delay, the psalmist cried out to God, expecting that God would answer in God's timing.

Verses 13 and 16 reveal that the psalmist's expectation of God's answer was based on the psalmist's understanding of the mercy and lovingkindness of God. Such a depth of understanding had grown out of experience.

The psalmist continued to cry out to God for help because he remembered times in the past when God had come through and delivered him from trouble. Without that confidence from experience, the psalmist surely would have given up on crying out to God. It was thus not *whether* God would help that weighed on the psalmist but *when* help would come.

Few aspects of the Christian walk frustrate and stretch the faith of believers more than the difference between our sense of urgency and God's timing in sending relief. There seems to be an implication that the psalmist knew and accepted the fact that God occasionally allows us to go through difficult times, and thus the psalmist was asking that God not allow him to be overcome by his enemies and circumstances. He was weary of his struggles and asked that God answer before his resolve failed and his enemies claimed victory. He was calling out to God because all human sources of relief and sympathy had failed, and he desired that God be shown to be the source for certain deliverance.

Verses 17–18 appear to be the heart of the entire psalm as the psalmist declared his total dependence on God by calling for God to redeem him. He knew that it was only through God's actions that the psalmist had any hope.

Cry for God's Judgment (69:22–29)

Beginning in verse 22, the reader sees the fully human heart of the psalmist as he spelled out the specific punishments he desired for God to hand out to his enemies. In these verses the psalmist certainly seemed

HESED

The Hebrew term in Psalm 69:16 that is translated "love" (NIV84) or "lovingkindness" (NASB) is *hesed*. This word is one of the most theologically significant terms in the Old Testament and speaks of the absolute faithfulness of God's love. Often connected with God's covenant with his people, the word expresses the quality in the heart of God that assures that God will never break that relationship.

to forget the call to love his enemies. But in the call for revenge against his oppressors, these verses show the psalmist's complete honesty before God. Such feelings are a part of our human nature, and God knows even these thoughts.

Such verses are often referred to as *imprecatory*, and some wish to soften words they see as inappropriate sentiments for the biblical text. Some suggest that the writer did not take joy in the ideas expressed but knew that sometimes God's punishment is severe.

Explaining away the clear message in such a manner seems unnecessary. Indeed, the fact that the Bible does so often present a fully honest portrayal of the actions and feelings of even the heroes allows the reader, who often acts and feels the same way, to fully relate and thereby learn from the text on a deeper level. Haven't we all at times desired the complete destruction of those who seem to oppose us?

This psalm assures us that it is acceptable to voice these desires to God. As we are fully honest before God, God can move in and change our focus as he did for the psalmist.

Confident Exclamation of Praise (69:30–36)

Hope broke through the psalmist's crisis, and praise erupted from the psalmist's heart. Notice that this was a cry of praise for God's action before the deliverance had come. As the psalmist cried out to God, he drew closer to God. As he drew closer to God, his concern shifted from his circumstances to God's constant care for God's oppressed people.

The psalmist was reminded that the mercy and lovingkindness on which he had based his plea earlier in the psalm were not just passive qualities of God but were active characteristics that are on continual display as God hears and delivers his people.

Earlier in the psalm, the psalmist had expressed concern that his life not cause others to stumble. Now the psalmist stated that when others saw how God moved in his life in rescuing him from the flood waters, they would be strengthened in their faith. Thus this psalm has presented the reader with the move from desperation to declaration. Such can happen to anyone who takes his or her complaints to God and in full humility and honesty pours them out and trusts that God will answer in God's time.

Implications for Today

Every person experiences times in life when people and circumstances make life difficult. While we might wish otherwise, believers are not immune. When those times come in the life of believers, we know that we can pray about them, but we often fail to do so until small issues become a flood of problems. When we do cry out to God for help and God does not immediately remove the trouble, we often begin to seek our own solution. This usually only leads us deeper into frustration and magnifies the feeling that the problems will overwhelm us.

Psalm 69 teaches us that God welcomes even our complaints as we cry out to him. Furthermore, God promises to handle our complaints in his own timing. If we will confidently bring our problems to God without doubt, we will not be overcome by people or circumstances. In addition, as we continue to bring our needs to God, we draw closer to God and find that even in waiting for an answer we lose our frustration as our heart sings songs of praise.

QUESTIONS

1. Has there been a time when you wrestled with your prayers and God's timing in answering? What happened?

2. How do you feel about the idea of complaining or questioning God in prayer?

3. When was the last time that honest prayer moved you from desperation to declaration? How did it change the situation?

4. In relation to the difficulties of life, what message does your life send to others?

Testifying of God's Security and Deliverance

FOCAL TEXT
Psalm 91

BACKGROUND
Psalm 91

MAIN IDEA
God provides security and deliverance in even the most threatening situations so that God's people need have no fear.

QUESTION TO EXPLORE
How can we deal with our fears?

STUDY AIM
To summarize the psalmist's testimony of how God provided security and deliverance and to testify of God's provision of security and deliverance in my life

QUICK READ
Psalm 91 describes the security and peace of those who put their complete trust in God.

Soon after our first child turned two, a friend gave us tickets to the circus. Our seats were in the front row at the back edge of the ring, right where all the performing animals entered.

My daughter's attention was riveted by the clowns' antics, and she did not notice that the elephants were arriving until they suddenly loomed before us. With a scream, Joy threw her arms around my neck and buried her face in my shoulder. No matter that the animals were many times my size, our little girl felt secure in my embrace until the beasts passed safely to the opposite side of the arena.

My baby looked to me for help when she felt threatened, but she didn't understand how truly frail my protection was. If one of the elephants had turned on us, we both might have died. In dramatic contrast, God's power to save has no limits. The psalmist described the confidence and hope of those who place their full trust in God's sovereign strength.

PSALM 91

1 He who dwells in the shelter of the Most High
    will rest in the shadow of the Almighty.
2 I will say of the LORD, "He is my refuge and my fortress,
    my God, in whom I trust."
3 Surely he will save you from the fowler's snare
    and from the deadly pestilence.
4 He will cover you with his feathers,
    and under his wings you will find refuge;
    his faithfulness will be your shield and rampart.
5 You will not fear the terror of night,
    nor the arrow that flies by day,
6 nor the pestilence that stalks in the darkness,
    nor the plague that destroys at midday.
7 A thousand may fall at your side,
    ten thousand at your right hand,
    but it will not come near you.
8 You will only observe with your eyes
    and see the punishment of the wicked.
9 If you make the Most High your dwelling—
    even the LORD, who is my refuge—

¹⁰ then no harm will befall you,
> no disaster will come near your tent.
¹¹ For he will command his angels concerning you
> to guard you in all your ways;
¹² they will lift you up in their hands,
> so that you will not strike your foot against a stone.
¹³ You will tread upon the lion and the cobra;
> you will trample the great lion and the serpent.
¹⁴ "Because he loves me," says the LORD, "I will rescue him;
> I will protect him, for he acknowledges my name.
¹⁵ He will call upon me, and I will answer him;
> I will be with him in trouble,
> I will deliver him and honor him.
¹⁶ With long life will I satisfy him
> and show him my salvation."

Quotations of Psalm 91 in the New Testament

Matthew 4:6; Luke 4:10–11

Words of Assurance (91:1–2)

Ancient writers did not use the punctuation marks we depend on for adding meaning to our words. Where we might insert an exclamation point for emphasis, the Hebrew scribes of old instead used repetition to strengthen a word or phrase. This practice was most strongly evident in their poetry.

People generally recognize rhyme as a characteristic of many poetic forms. Biblical poets used that device, as well. But where English-speaking poets rhyme sounds, the Hebrew psalmists used rhyming ideas. This created a parallel structure for the more important words and phrases, which were reinforced with synonyms and repeated for emphasis.

Psalm 91 is a good example of this parallel structure. If we break the first verse into two parts and examine them side-by-side, the repeated ideas become evident. "He who dwells . . . will rest." The word "dwells" implies residing or staying. In the second half of the verse, the word translated "rest" is more accurately rendered *abide* or *remain*. The two synonyms—"dwells" and "rest"—work together to create an image of permanent residence in God's presence.

Consider the next repeated idea. The words "shelter" and "shadow" carry connotations of care, protection, and safety. The "shadow" here represents a place of safety similar to that of a chick hidden beneath a parent's wings. God provides a place of safety that shelters his people from outside threats and shields them from danger.

The third focal concept of the verse emerges in the person of God himself, who is dually described as "the Most High" and "the Almighty." Individually, each of these names describes God's power and invincibility. When used together, they build a profile of incomparable strength and might. Nothing can move this God. Nothing can threaten or challenge him. He is absolute sovereign, with absolute power. Whatever he protects will stay protected.

In the space of one verse, the psalmist has established the idea that any person who lives with God will enjoy the absolute safety of God's unmatched power. Verse 2 follows with the reader's obvious response. The response acknowledges God as the source of rescue from an imperiled condition by saying, "He is my refuge and my fortress." Note the repeated concept in the writer's synonyms. The "refuge" offers a safe place to hide from danger, and the "fortress" represents impenetrable protection. Whatever the threat, it cannot touch those who have staked their trust in the God who is their home.

Structure and Meaning (91:3–4)

As a literary form, poetry can often express deep emotion more effectively than prose because the language is so condensed. Bounded by limited line counts, poets must avoid generalities and choose strong words that target precise meanings.

Ancient psalmists understood this constraint. They combined structure and language to achieve spiritual purpose in their songs. This principle is evident in the progression of Psalm 91.

PARALLELISM IN HEBREW POETRY

An outstanding characteristic of Hebrew poetry is parallelism. There are different types of parallelism, but two of the easiest to recognize are synonymous and antithetical. In synonymous parallelism, the second line restates the first so the main idea is repeated. This is apparent in Psalm 70:1–2:

> Hasten, O God, to save me;
>> O LORD, come quickly to help me.
> May those who seek my life
>> be put to shame and confusion;
> may all who desire my ruin
>> be turned back in disgrace.

Antithetical parallelism uses opposite or contrasting ideas to make a point. Psalm 75:10 is a good example:

> I will cut off the horns of all the wicked,
>> but the horns of the righteous will be lifted up.

The psalmists used parallelism to emphasize truths about God and encourage readers to ponder them. Thinking of different ways to express the same spiritual principle helps clarify it. When you read biblical psalms, watch for parallelism and repetition. Consider how awareness of them might help keep your thoughts focused on God's attributes.

Having established that God protects and defends those who trust in him, the writer built his readers' confidence in the truth by outlining specific details of God's care. He began in verse 3 by using images that were familiar to people of that time period. They would have understood a "fowler's snare" to represent hidden dangers laid by enemies. The threat of "pestilence" was even more terrifying to them, for disease epidemics caused widespread death and destruction beyond any human interference or control. Yet verse 4 gives assurance that God's people could be assured of complete protection from any danger.

In verse 4, the psalmist completed the picture from verse 1 that hinted toward God's covering wings. He also introduced a new element, that

---

FACING AN OVERWHELMING SITUATION

When faced with an overwhelming situation, try these steps to help
focus your prayers:

1. Acknowledge God's presence and ability to hear and
   respond.
2. Describe how you perceive the situation.
3. State what is true about God's character, nature, attributes,
   and activity.
4. Assess how God is involved in the problem.
5. Seek an eternal perspective; ask for God's help to see
   circumstances through his eyes and to wait for him to reveal
   his purpose.

---

of the Lord's "faithfulness." The Almighty God who has power to safe-
guard his people can be trusted to do it. His defense will never fail.
God's faithfulness is an unmovable barricade, a bulwark against menac-
ing forces or events.

Notice the structure the writer used to build his case. With every
escalation of threat he responded with an answering revelation of God's
greater power to save. Then he followed with the only logical conclu-
sion left to the reader. Since no danger can penetrate God's perfect and
unfailing defenses, no reason is left for fear.

No Cause for Alarm (91:5–10)

With fear of evil spirits so prevalent in ancient cultures, it is probable
that the night terror in verse 5 refers to demonic activity. This is paral-
leled in the next verse's description of the "pestilence that stalks in the
darkness." The potential for panic grows as peril increases. Evil spirits
are stalking and terrorizing their prey; arrows are flying from enemies
either human or supernatural; plague, perhaps the result of demonic

curses, is destroying indiscriminately. The numbers of dead and dying are increasing. Death, mayhem, and destruction are on every side.

But wait, don't get excited, the writer soothed. In verse 9 he circled back to the psalm's beginning. *Remember your hope,* he reminded readers. *If you have made God Most High your dwelling, then none of the violence will affect you. You will witness the judgment of those who refused God's offer of sanctuary. They will fall victim to every threat outlined in the previous verses, but there is no terror for the one who takes refuge in God's protection. None of those dangers will come anywhere near those who trust in God.*

The assurance in verse 10 that "no harm will befall you" or "come near your tent" should be considered within its context. If we have taken up residence within God's presence, then we will have *pitched our tent there,* so to speak. The image here is not a bubble of protection that follows if we wander away from God's house. Rather, it is the complete immersion in God's Spirit that shields us from outside threat. We can't plant our hearts just anywhere and expect to enjoy the same degree of peace and confidence that comes with total submission to God's sovereignty.

Divine Relationship (91:11–16)

To confirm just how effective and complete God's protection is, the psalmist introduced a new and surprising element. Angels had appeared throughout Israel's history, acting as messengers (Genesis 16:9–10), divine warriors (Numbers 22:31), and ministering spirits (1 Kings 19:5–7). Verse 11 speaks of angels as guarding God's people. These spiritual servants act under God's authority, responding to God's direct command, and represent God's divine hand on believers wherever they go.

Keeping in mind that poetry as a literary genre is characterized by figurative imagery, there is no reason to interpret verses 12–13 literally. If verse 4 does not compel us to believe that God actually has feathered wings, then likewise we will not assume that verse 13 grants us license to take up hand-to-hand combat with lions or go around stomping on poisonous snakes.

The animals named by the psalmist in verse 13 posed real threats to the people of his day. The lion was known for aggression and frontal attacks, while the serpent represented hidden peril. Both of these recalled the same types of dangers outlined in previous verses. But the context in which they appear is that of God's encompassing care. God extends his protection over every part of life, from traveling the stony roads of ancient Palestine to encountering unexpected trials along the way. Mortal threats hold no terror for a heart fully committed to God.

The structure of verse 14 stands out from those that precede it. The repeated verbs and nouns in the two lines of verse 13, for example, are parallel: "tread" and "trample"; "lion" and "lion"; "cobra" and "serpent." But suddenly the psalmist switched to a different structure for verse 14. Observe that the verse begins and ends with the same idea, and the secondary ideas meet in the middle.

Note God's promises in the second and third phrases of verse 14. He will "rescue" and "protect." These are bordered on either side by the conditions that prompt God's response. God saves the one who loves him, the one who acknowledges his name. This becomes the key to the whole song. We love and acknowledge God because God is "Most High," because God is "Almighty," and because God is faithful. God responds to our love and reverence by lavishing his care, protection, and blessing on us. He listens and answers when we call on him. He will never leave or forsake us, and we will fully experience the peace and freedom of life without fear in his presence.

Applying This Lesson to Life

History rings with stories of divine deliverance, inspirational testimonies of people saved from perilous situations. Many have pointed to Psalm 91 as witness to the Lord's supernatural protection. But what about martyrs who weren't delivered? What about faithful Christians who died violently at the hands of unbelievers? Do their deaths invalidate the psalm's promises?

As mortal beings we are necessarily concerned with our physical welfare. But the threat of danger or disease does not negate God's protection. We perceive our circumstances through a lens of worldly limitations. We must remember that God relates to us from an eternal perspective.

The whole focus of Psalm 91 is more the condition of our hearts than the safety of our bodies. If we fully invest our trust in God's sovereignty, then fear will disappear from our lives. Resting in the knowledge that God is continually working for our eternal good removes the element of uncertainty and alarm from our hearts.

QUESTIONS

1. How might the psalmist have described our trust in God and God's protection over us if he were writing prose instead of poetry?

2. How is it possible to spiritually "dwell" in God's presence when our bodies are stuck in a physical world?

3. When the psalmist wrote of pestilence, arrows, lions, or serpents, he was calling up images that terrified the people of his time. What frightens you most? What threats cause anxiety in your life?

4. How can trust in God's sovereignty remove fear from your life?

5. What steps might you take to strengthen your trust in God and to practice submission to his lordship?

FOCAL TEXT
Psalm 95

BACKGROUND
Psalm 95

MAIN IDEA
Genuine worship of God cannot occur without faithful obedience to God.

QUESTION TO EXPLORE
How closely related is your worship on Sunday to your life on Monday?

STUDY AIM
To evaluate my life by both my worship of God and my obedience to God

QUICK READ
Although praise and worship may generate joy in the hearts of believers, these acts mean nothing to God unless our lives are fully committed to him.

LESSON TWELVE
Let Us Worship, Let Us Obey

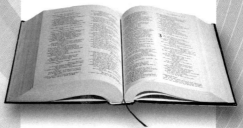

The sign-up sheet for praise team auditions was full. Dozens of students at our Christian high school were trying out for the ensemble that led singing in weekly chapel services.

Working on a bulletin board just inside my classroom door, I could hear students talking together in the hallway. One conversation in particular caught my attention. "I really need to get on the praise team," a girl was saying, "so I can get out of chemistry. All the song leaders can leave fourth period twenty minutes early on Wednesdays to set up for chapel." I later was relieved to hear that she did not make the team.

That girl was not the only student, or even adult, for that matter, whose heart was in the wrong place. Almost every week I saw teenagers texting or playing video games on their cell phones during the chapel talk, when only moments before they had been singing praise choruses with uplifted hands. Do we adults sometimes engage in similar behavior?

Worship is more than just words and music. The writer of Psalm 95 warns that our expressions of praise are worthless if our hearts are not right before God.

PSALM 95

1 Come, let us sing for joy to the LORD;
   let us shout aloud to the Rock of our salvation.
2 Let us come before him with thanksgiving
   and extol him with music and song.
3 For the LORD is the great God,
   the great King above all gods.
4 In his hand are the depths of the earth,
   and the mountain peaks belong to him.
5 The sea is his, for he made it,
   and his hands formed the dry land.
6 Come, let us bow down in worship,
   let us kneel before the LORD our Maker;
7 for he is our God
   and we are the people of his pasture,
   the flock under his care.
   Today, if you hear his voice,

⁸ do not harden your hearts as you did at Meribah,
   as you did that day at Massah in the desert,
⁹ where your fathers tested and tried me,
   though they had seen what I did.
¹⁰ For forty years I was angry with that generation;
   I said, "They are a people whose hearts go astray,
   and they have not known my ways."
¹¹ So I declared on oath in my anger,
   "They shall never enter my rest."

Quotations of Psalm 95 in the New Testament

Hebrews 3:7–11, 15; 4:3, 5, 7

Elements of Praise (95:1–5)

What have you heard parents say to praise their children? How about these: *You did a good job! You really worked hard to finish that project. You did your best. You didn't give up.*

The real purpose of praise is to acknowledge what is true about someone. Whether in the context of parent to child, teacher to student, boss to employee, or friend to friend, the person on the receiving end of praise feels affirmed and gratified that his or her efforts have been recognized and appreciated.

God does not depend on our praise for his happiness. He is fully sufficient within himself and needs nothing from us. But it pleases God when we acknowledge who he is and what he has done. He expects to receive praise because he deserves it. The glory and power reflected in the works of God's hand are too wondrous to ignore. And as we recount God's mighty acts, the joy of God's love and care wells up in our hearts and spills over in adoration.

Although praise and worship are closely related, subtle differences separate them. The writer of Psalm 95 structured the song so that one leads to another. The psalmist prepared for worship by focusing first on praise.

With a song and joyful shout, the psalmist identified God as the object of praise by acknowledging his divine attributes (Psalm 95:1). The psalmist chose word images that evoked a broad range of responses. God as our Rock, for example, encompasses God's steadfastness, strength, and protection. Then God is acclaimed as the source of our salvation. No matter the peril—betrayal, disease, catastrophe, spiritual impoverishment—God is the One who saves.

Within the context of polytheism that dominated ancient cultures, the psalmist addressed God's position as ultimate Sovereign of the world. The deities venerated by other people groups could not compare to *Yahweh* (Ps. 95:3). He is superior to, greater than, and King above all gods. If anyone doubted this truth, the writer pointed to the evidence in creation (95:4–5). Just see what God the King has done. The earth belongs to him; he created and rules it from the deepest crevices to the tallest mountains. Contrary to pagan assumptions, no foreign deities could reside in the heights, for the mountains and hills fell within God's domain alone. He formed the land with his own hand as a potter molds clay. The oceans submitted to his authority, resting within the boundaries he assigned.

All of these things are true of God, sang the writer. His power and majesty, strength and dominion, care and salvation compel our praise and fill us with joy in his presence.

Where Worship Begins (95:6–7)

The process of naming God's attributes begins to generate a sense of awe at his greatness. Praise establishes God's worthiness, what is sometimes described as God's *otherness*. It recognizes his place above and outside of linear time and finite space.

At this point praise merges with worship (95:6). Where praise acknowledges that God is sovereign and deserves adoration, worship moves people toward submission to God. It is one thing to say that God is King, but another to kneel before God and yield to God's absolute authority.

In the call to worship in verse 6, the writer used a different term from the one with which he began the psalm. Many Bible interpreters view the call to "come" in the first two verses, literally rendered *let us come*

THE PSALMS—SONGS OF WORSHIP

Psalms were to the Israelites what hymns, choir anthems, and praise choruses are to modern church services. They were the songs of worship. Different types of psalms were incorporated into various occasions. The greater number of these were *laments*, used when individuals or communities cried out to God for help in distress. *Songs of thanksgiving* and *songs of confidence* expressed gratitude for God's blessings or help and assurance of his deliverance. *Pilgrim psalms* were sung by worshipers traveling to Jerusalem, and *wisdom psalms* instructed people in right conduct and urged obedience to his law. These and other psalms played an important role in Hebrew rituals, ceremonies, and festivals even into New Testament times.

Psalm 95 is an example of an *enthronement psalm. Enthronement psalms* were most commonly used in festivals celebrating the New Year, during which a service was held to acclaim God's rule over Israel and enthrone him as King. The purpose of the psalms in these rituals was to proclaim God's power and sovereignty and to exhort Israel toward covenant obedience.

before his face, as an invitation to enter the temple. The opening verses of this psalm are clearly a call to praise (95:1–2).

The word "come" in verse 6 means *enter*, indicating a progressive action. Tethered to the synonyms that follow—"worship," "bow down," "kneel"—this exhortation is stronger and deeper than the first call to sing thanks to the Lord. The worshipers had moved past the point of merely extolling God's attributes. Now they must realize their utter unworthiness before the One who created them and prostrate themselves before him.

The act of prostration before rulers was common in ancient cultures. This involved lying face down on the floor at the king's feet. With the person's eyes averted and neck exposed, a swordsman could easily sever the head without encountering any resistance. The position symbolically implied that the prostrate person's life belonged to the sovereign. The person was yielding himself to the king's authority over him, even to the point of death.

This is the true heart of worship: *I am nothing; God is all. God designed and made me, and I belong to him. His authority compels my obedience.*

His will must become my will, so that I desire only what he determines for me.

This attitude moves beyond praise to lodge in the heart and mind. Genuine worship is not dependent on emotions but is evidenced in changed outlook and behavior.

Verse 7 clarifies the relationship we share with the God we worship. He is not an indifferent deity so far above as to be removed from any interaction with us. Rather, God is intricately involved in our lives in the same way a shepherd stays with and cares for his flock. The image of a shepherd conveys a sense of leadership, provision, and protection. As the sheep in the Shepherd's possession, our path is sure, our needs are met, and we dwell in safety. Under such conditions, the worship we offer is not a toilsome duty to placate an angry god, but flows from a wellspring of devotion and gratitude.

Empty Words (95:7d–11)

During our years in Asia, a missionary friend's parents came from America for a visit. When our two families spent a day sightseeing together, I noticed his elderly father often addressed in rapid English the nationals he encountered. Finally the son pulled his father aside

---

GETTING SOMETHING OUT OF CHURCH

Have you ever heard anyone comment, "I didn't get anything out of that church service today," or "That sermon just didn't do anything for me." Some people seem to judge the validity of a worship experience by the emotional response it evoked.

A more accurate standard of measure should include these questions:

- Was my heart submissive to God?
- Did any barriers of sin or guilt corrupt the sincerity of my praise?
- Was God the focus of my attention and my thoughts?
- Was God glorified in every element of the experience?

and explained, "Dad, they can't understand you. They don't speak English."

"Oh, they understand, all right," his father replied. "They just pretend like they don't."

Just as the man's words were empty of meaning for the Asians who heard them, praise from empty hearts is meaningless to God. God said in Isaiah 29:13, "These people come near to me with their mouth and honor me with their lips, but their hearts are far from me. Their worship of me is made up only of rules taught by men."

Don't let that happen, the psalmist pleaded, speaking on God's behalf at the end of verse 7. *Don't repeat the mistakes of the Israelites who wandered in the wilderness.* The last four verses of the psalm recall their stubborn arrogance. Instead of being grateful for God's deliverance and provision on their escape from Egypt, the people continually complained and demanded more and more from him. After witnessing God's power, they should have knelt before him in humble submission, but their attitudes were anything but obedient. They refused to acknowledge the sincerity of his care, calling for him to prove it to them again and again.

In returning disloyalty for divine provision, fickleness for God's faithfulness, and perverseness for his protection, it is understandable how the Israelites forfeited God's favor. His love turned to disgust. The blessings God intended for his people were replaced by punishment.

This section of the psalm stands out in sharp contrast to the first seven verses. After showcasing God's sovereign might and constructing an argument for genuine praise and true worship, the writer pointed to a case study revealing the consequences of rebellious hearts. The psalmist seems to be implying, *I've told you what you should do to honor God; here's what you can expect to happen if you don't. Think about it.*

The Bible contains many accounts of people who turned from God and made unwise choices. The purpose of these passages is to instruct us. It is foolish not to learn from others' mistakes. In this psalm the writer held up two examples for us, one good and one bad. The first inspires joy, the second heartache. One immerses us in God's pleasure, while the other earns his anger. Taken together, both sections urge the reader toward relating to God with the reverence and honor God deserves.

Applying This Lesson to Life

Have you ever found yourself singing songs in church while your mind was far away? How can we guard against going through the motions of worship with wrong motives or empty words? Prayer can help. Before approaching any time of praise or worship, we should ask God to prepare our hearts for it. If God is the one directing our thoughts, then we will accomplish God's purpose for the experience.

A true encounter with God will always change us in some way, whether by a quiet revelation of God's presence, a deeper understanding of God's will, a new spiritual insight, or a conviction of sin or weakness that compels an obedient response. If we're missing that, then we need to spend more time listening for God's voice. It's easy to miss the Spirit's holy whisper, even in church, if we're distracted by other things around us.

QUESTIONS

1. Why do you think the psalmist went all the way back to creation as the reference point for praising God's power instead of focusing on more recent acts of divine intervention?

2. What is the relationship between articulating God's acts and experiencing joy because of them?

3. What are the differences between praise and worship?

4. Recall a time when you experienced a deeply meaningful worship experience. What impact did it have on you? How did it affect your spiritual growth?

5. How can we judge whether we are trying to compromise with God by justifying our questionable actions or are being truly obedient? How does obedience affect our ability to worship?

FOCAL TEXT
Psalm 118

BACKGROUND
Psalm 118

MAIN IDEA
The psalmist's experience with the steadfast love of the Lord provided numerous reasons for giving thanks to him.

QUESTIONS TO EXPLORE
How has God demonstrated his steadfast love to you? How do you plan to respond?

STUDY AIM
To identify reasons for giving thanks to the Lord and to offer my thanks to him

QUICK READ
This psalm is a hymn of thanksgiving to God for salvation and victory.

LESSON THIRTEEN
Give Thanks for the Lord's Steadfast Love

Our family was sued after my teenaged son's involvement in an accident. The case dragged on for six years before going to trial, and at times we worried it would bankrupt us. We were relieved and grateful when the jury finally found in our favor. We couldn't thank God enough for his deliverance or for the strength he supplied for enduring the ordeal. Perhaps you could cite times in your life when you felt almost overwhelmed by some difficulty but at last deliverance came and you were grateful to God.

Throughout its history, Israel experienced attacks from many different enemies. At times Hebrew kings depended on their own strength or sought help from neighboring allies to withstand invasion. Those attempts ended in disaster. But when the people turned to God, God responded with amazing acts of protection and deliverance. At those times the nation poured out thanks to the Lord. Psalm 118 is an example of the hymns the Israelites sang in thanks to God after God gave them victory over their enemies.

PSALM 118

1 Give thanks to the LORD, for he is good;
   his love endures forever.
2 Let Israel say:
   "His love endures forever."
3 Let the house of Aaron say:
   "His love endures forever."
4 Let those who fear the LORD say:
   "His love endures forever."
5 In my anguish I cried to the LORD,
   and he answered by setting me free.
6 The LORD is with me; I will not be afraid.
   What can man do to me?
7 The LORD is with me; he is my helper.
   I will look in triumph on my enemies.
8 It is better to take refuge in the LORD
   than to trust in man.
9 It is better to take refuge in the LORD
   than to trust in princes.

10 All the nations surrounded me,
   but in the name of the LORD I cut them off.
11 They surrounded me on every side,
   but in the name of the LORD I cut them off.
12 They swarmed around me like bees,
   but they died out as quickly as burning thorns;
   in the name of the LORD I cut them off.
13 I was pushed back and about to fall,
   but the LORD helped me.
14 The LORD is my strength and my song;
   he has become my salvation.
15 Shouts of joy and victory
   resound in the tents of the righteous:
   "The LORD's right hand has done mighty things!
16   The LORD's right hand is lifted high;
   the LORD's right hand has done mighty things!"
17 I will not die but live,
   and will proclaim what the LORD has done.
18 The LORD has chastened me severely,
   but he has not given me over to death.
19 Open for me the gates of righteousness;
   I will enter and give thanks to the LORD.
20 This is the gate of the LORD
   through which the righteous may enter.
21 I will give you thanks, for you answered me;
   you have become my salvation.
22 The stone the builders rejected
   has become the capstone;
23 the LORD has done this,
   and it is marvelous in our eyes.
24 This is the day the LORD has made;
   let us rejoice and be glad in it.
25 O LORD, save us;
   O LORD, grant us success.
26 Blessed is he who comes in the name of the LORD.
   From the house of the LORD we bless you.

²⁷ The LORD is God,
    and he has made his light shine upon us.
    With boughs in hand, join in the festal procession
    up to the horns of the altar.
²⁸ You are my God, and I will give you thanks;
    you are my God, and I will exalt you.
²⁹ Give thanks to the LORD, for he is good;
    his love endures forever.

Quotations of Psalm 118 in the New Testament

Matthew 21:9, 42; 23:39; Mark 11:9–10; 12:10–11;
Luke 13:35; 19:38; 20:17; John 12:13;
Acts 4:11; Hebrews 13:6; 1 Peter 2:7

A Prayer of Thanks (118:1–4)

Psalm 118 is the last in a group called the *Hallel Psalms*. These psalms recalled God's deliverance from Egypt and were used during Jewish festivals. Families usually sang Psalms 113—114 before the annual Passover meal, and Psalms 115—118 after it was finished. Psalm 118 might also have been used as a processional hymn during the Feast of Tabernacles. The song recalls God's great power in defending Israel and granting victory over its enemies.

The psalmist began by summoning everyone in the nation, from the greatest to the least, to give thanks to God. First he called the king, who is symbolically represented by the name of Israel (Psalm 118:2). Next came the priests and Levites from the line of Aaron, who were charged with the nation's religious leadership. Finally he beckoned all the people to assemble and join in the prayer to acknowledge God's love and care.

This psalm is built around the Hebrew concept of *hesed*, a word that is repeated in every verse of Psalm 118:1–4, translated as "love" (NIV84) or "lovingkindness" (NASB). This term encompasses God's unfailing and steadfast love, which is manifested in grace, mercy, and goodness to his people. God's attributes of mercy and goodness lead him to lavish an eternal and unchanging love on his people, even though they have not earned it and cannot deserve it. So the song of thanksgiving is not just an expression of gratitude for victory, but also for God's faithful loving-kindness, the *hesed* God pours on his people.

Threats of Peril (118:5–14)

The writer used figurative opposites to set the tone in verse 5. He described how he cried out, and God answered. He was distressed, and God set him free from distress. The word "anguish," or *distress,* here literally means *a small, confined space,* while the meaning of "setting me free" is *a large, roomy place.* This does not imply that the psalmist was imprisoned, but the connotation is that God released him from restrictive options imposed by his enemies or circumstances.

Again in verse 6, the psalmist contrasted God's power with the frailty of human threats. The idea is repeated in a parallel line in the next verse. With God beside him, he would prevail over anyone who meant him harm. *So then,* the writer continued in verses 8–9, *if God's power overcomes people's threats, isn't it more logical to trust in God than to trust in people?*

The first-person speaker in verses 10–14 was probably the king, who represented all of Israel. To describe the intensity of the danger the king faced, the psalmist used an exaggerated picture of all pagan nations on earth opposing the king and the nation. The speaker was under fierce attack, threatened by certain defeat, and yet God rescued him. He testified that his strength in battle came from God alone.

A Song of Victory (118:15–21)

A small international school in Asia had a good basketball team because of one star player. As long as his teammates fed him the ball, he drilled one basket after another, hitting from anywhere on the court. But if he got sick and missed a game, the other players struggled to keep up with their opponents. The team won games only if their star was present.

Just as the school team attributed all their wins to their best player, the psalmist even more joyfully acknowledged God's hand in Israel's victory over its enemies. The "tents of the righteous" in verse 15 represent the people of God who submit to his authority and obey his laws. The

CAPSTONES

Ancient builders used capstones (literally, *head of the corner*) in different ways. Often a capstone was a cornerstone in a foundation, placed where two rows came together to anchor and align them. At other times it was a large stone used as a lintel over a doorway, or a keystone that completed an arch. Sometimes the last stone placed at the top of a completed structure was also called the capstone.

The capstone was commonly perceived as the most important or dedicatory stone. It often held everything together. It is not surprising, then, that some ancient references identified religious leaders as cornerstones of their people (see Isaiah 19:13; Zechariah 10:4). This symbol carried over into Jesus' day. The temple priests and teachers of the law perceived themselves as cornerstones of Hebrew faith. That is why Jesus' claim to be the cornerstone of Psalm 118:22 was so troubling to them. He implied that the Scriptures converged on him as their foundation, thus stripping the religious leaders of their authority.

image that follows of God's "right hand" is a symbolic reference to God's mighty power, against which no enemy could stand.

In verse 17 the speaker, again probably the king, was testifying how God chose to spare his life when from all appearances he should not have survived his battles. He further acknowledged in the next verse that God had a purpose for allowing him to experience the trial. Receiving the Lord's discipline humbled him, but it also encouraged him to greater faith and obedience. Now he intended to stand in a public place and share his experiences and insights with the people.

The psalmist recorded the exchange between the king and the temple gatekeepers in verse 19. The king called out a request to enter the temple for the purpose of giving thanks to God. In the following verses they responded that only God's faithful followers might pass through his gates. This is an exhortation to self-examination, to ensure that the speaker had cleansed his heart from any barriers of guilt that might taint the purity of his worship.

Assured of his clean conscience, the speaker entered God's sanctuary. He now declared his thanks to God for answering his prayers and giving him salvation.

God's Purpose Prevails (118:22–29)

Some Old Testament verses are difficult to understand within their own context but become clearer in the light of New Testament interpretation. Verses 22–23 may fall into that category. The psalmist spoke of how the Lord's intervention could change a person's perspective. Using a construction metaphor, he described how the builders of a large structure dismissed a stone because they considered it worthless. But their evaluation changed when they finally recognized it as the building's capstone, the most important of all. The point was not that the stone's value increased, but that God worked in the builders' hearts to enable better understanding of the stone's worth. Within the context of this psalm, the metaphor probably illustrates how Israel rose to stand out among all the pagan nations that rejected her, and God was the one who brought it about. Israel was witness to the wonderful thing God had done.

From a New Testament perspective, these verses are prophetic references to Jesus Christ. He was rejected by men who didn't recognize his lordship and plotted his execution, but then he rose to become the sole means of salvation from eternal death. Peter referred to this passage when speaking before the Sanhedrin (Acts 4:11) and to encourage the faith of believers (1 Peter 2:7). Jesus himself used it to rebuke the stubborn hypocrisy of religious leaders of his day (Matthew 21:42; Mark 12:10–11; Luke 20:17).

Although the words of verse 24 are often sung in worship services today, their connotation within the psalm's context is different from that of many modern praise choruses that use these words. In the psalm, the statement, "This is the day the LORD has made" implies that all of the events that have taken place were orchestrated by God. That is, *this is the day in which we celebrate the Lord's victory; he is the reason we're here.*

The lines "save us" and "grant us success" in verse 25 are prayers for continued victory over enemies and for blessing and prosperity. The theme of blessing is carried over into the next verse. Anyone who is faithful and righteous—those who have been judged worthy to enter God's house to worship—is already living under God's blessing. From a full heart, that person will in turn bless the Lord.

Here is another hint forward to Christ. In Matthew 21:9; Mark 11:9; Luke 19:38; and John 12:13, the people of Jerusalem acclaimed Jesus as the embodiment of the person described in Psalm 118:26. He was not

GOD'S STEADFAST LOVE TODAY

As a young boy, G. was forced to quit school when his mother became too ill to work. He took over her job washing and ironing clothes. Ten years later, American missionaries found him and enrolled him in classes they had established for Filipinos who had left school for economic reasons. The patience and love he received from Christian teachers changed his life. The day he graduated with a fifth-grade diploma, he continually thanked God. What began as a personal tragedy became the gateway to salvation for G. and his family.

Does your life reflect God's steadfast love for others?

just any pilgrim intent on worshiping in God's house; he is *the* righteous King, who bears the full favor and authority of God. He comes in the power of the Lord, and God's blessing will fall on those who accompany him

Verse 27 contains another acknowledgement that God was the source of the nation's salvation and victory. The image of God's light shining over the people represented the blessings, prosperity, and victory God had bestowed on them. The festival procession, recognizable by flowering branches that were carried in to decorate the altar, demonstrated the outpouring of thanks and rejoicing for all God had done.

Once inside the temple, the king recognized God as the object of worship and once more offered thanks (Ps. 118:28). This was a formal, ceremonial expression of gratitude on behalf of the nation, as well as the king's personal declaration of trust in God.

The final verse reprises the first, representing a celebration of thanksgiving that is complete, lacking nothing. Therefore, it would be acceptable to God.

QUESTIONS

1. In what ways have you experienced God's power and victory in your life? How has God shown his faithfulness?

2. How do you express thanks to God for his blessings in your life?

3. What are some non-verbal means of demonstrating gratitude?

4. Why is it important to thank God for what God gives and does?

5. What factors may cause some people to neglect giving thanks to God?

6. In what ways can you strengthen your resolve to express gratitude to God? How can you be certain that the thanks you give is sincere?

FOCAL TEXT
John 20:1–18

BACKGROUND
John 20:1–18

MAIN IDEA
Jesus' resurrection confirms
his identity and mission
and calls us to follow him
and tell others about him.

QUESTIONS TO EXPLORE
How have you experienced
Jesus? How have you
told others?

STUDY AIM
To describe Mary Magdalene's
encounter with the risen
Jesus and to recall my own
experience with Jesus

QUICK READ
Mary Magdalene's encounter
with the risen Jesus serves
not only as a basis for our
faith but also compels us
to share our Christian
experience with others.

EASTER LESSON
Experiencing,
Believing, Telling

Some years ago, I had the wonderful opportunity to travel to the Holy Land and tour many of the places Jesus walked and lived. One of the tour stops was the site traditionally known as the burial place of Jesus. I was able to walk inside and see that the tomb was empty. This moment was so moving that I couldn't wait to get back home and tell everyone what I saw.

Have you ever had an experience that was so life-changing that you couldn't wait to tell somebody? That is the story of Mary Magdalene. Her message to the disciples of her life-changing experience on resurrection morning serves as an example to all Christians to eagerly share their faith in Jesus Christ. Our lesson explores the events of that morning as seen through Mary's encounter with the risen Jesus.[1]

JOHN 20:1–18

[1] Now on the first day of the week Mary Magdalene came early to the tomb, while it was still dark, and saw the stone already taken away from the tomb. [2] So she ran and came to Simon Peter and to the other disciple whom Jesus loved, and said to them, "They have taken away the Lord out of the tomb, and we do not know where they have laid Him." [3] So Peter and the other disciple went forth, and they were going to the tomb. [4] The two were running together; and the other disciple ran ahead faster than Peter and came to the tomb first; [5] and stooping and looking in, he saw the linen wrappings lying there; but he did not go in. [6] And so Simon Peter also came, following him, and entered the tomb; and he saw the linen wrappings lying there, [7] and the face-cloth which had been on His head, not lying with the linen wrappings, but rolled up in a place by itself. [8] So the other disciple who had first come to the tomb then also entered, and he saw and believed. [9] For as yet they did not understand the Scripture, that He must rise again from the dead. [10] So the disciples went away again to their own homes.

[11] But Mary was standing outside the tomb weeping; and so, as she wept, she stooped and looked into the tomb; [12] and she saw two angels in white sitting, one at the head and one at the feet,

where the body of Jesus had been lying. [13] And they said to her, "Woman, why are you weeping?" She said to them, "Because they have taken away my Lord, and I do not know where they have laid Him." [14] When she had said this, she turned around and saw Jesus standing there, and did not know that it was Jesus. [15] Jesus said to her, "Woman, why are you weeping? Whom are you seeking?" Supposing Him to be the gardener, she said to Him, "Sir, if you have carried Him away, tell me where you have laid Him, and I will take Him away." [16] Jesus said to her, "Mary!" She turned and said to Him in Hebrew, "Rabboni!" (which means, Teacher). [17] Jesus said to her, "Stop clinging to Me, for I have not yet ascended to the Father; but go to My brethren and say to them, 'I ascend to My Father and your Father, and My God and your God.'" [18] Mary Magdalene came, announcing to the disciples, "I have seen the Lord," and that He had said these things to her.

Mary's Eagerness (20:1)

John identifies Mary Magdalene as the first of Jesus' followers at the tomb Sunday morning. She had been one of the last to depart from the cross (John 19:25). John adds that she was there early, "while it was still dark" (20:1). The Greek word translated "early" is used to describe the fourth watch of the night.[2] The Romans divided the night into four periods or *watches*. These were 6 p.m. to 9 p.m., 9 p.m. to midnight, midnight to 3 a.m., and 3 a.m. to 6 a.m. (the fourth watch). So, sometime between 3 a.m. and sunrise, Mary Magdalene made her way to the tomb.

Most Bible scholars identify Mary Magdalene as the woman from whom Jesus cast out seven demons and who supported his ministry financially as mentioned in Luke 8:2–3. Since Mary was a common name in Jesus' time, the Gospel writers distinguished this Mary from the others by adding the name "Magdalene," thus noting she was from Magdala. Magdala is the Aramaic rendering of Migdol, a small town on the western shore of the Sea of Galilee.

Whereas Matthew, Mark, and Luke mention at least three other women who visited the tomb that morning, John mentions only Mary Magdalene (see Matthew 28:1; Mark 16:1; Luke 24:1, 10). This should not

FIRST-CENTURY TOMBS

Tombs in Jesus' time were typically an opening in a rock wall that was large enough to place a body in. Joseph of Arimathea and other affluent figures in society could afford larger tombs that a person could actually walk into. The tomb in which Jesus was buried likely was large enough to fit two to three people at a time. Tombs were sealed by rolling a large cartwheel-like stone in front of the opening. This large stone would roll into a groove in the ground and latch in place right at the entrance of the tomb. Once the heavy stone was latched in place, it was almost impossible to move. In some cases the tomb had to be sealed by cementing the huge stone to the walls of the entrance using hardening clay-like substance. These security measures were essential to protect tombs from being ransacked.

be viewed as a contradiction in that all the Gospels mention that Mary Magdalene went to the tomb that morning. John's mentioning only Mary Magdalene does not refute the probability of others being present simply because the Gospel writer chose to focus on her unique devotion. The possibility of the presence of other women can be seen in Mary's use of the plural "we" when addressing Simon Peter and "the other disciple whom Jesus loved" in John 20:2. It would not be considered unusual for a writer in the first century to highlight a particular personality in a group without mentioning the composition of the entire group.

Mary Magdalene was eager to ensure that Jesus' body received the proper burial treatment (Mark 16:1). Likely she could barely sleep that night, having witnessed the mode in which Joseph of Arimathea and Nicodemus quickly placed Jesus' body in the tomb on Friday so as to not violate the Sabbath laws. Her love and devotion to Jesus beckoned her to the tomb in the wee hours of the morning.

On her first visit, she was startled to see the stone had been removed from the entrance. She ran to tell Peter and the other disciple. When they heard the news, they ran to see for themselves. Notice the actions of Mary and the two disciples. Verse 2 states, "she ran." In verses 3–4, both disciples "were running together," but "the other disciple ran ahead faster than Peter and came to the tomb first." Why were they running? First, both Mary and the disciples were emotionally shaken by the news.

Their haste was possibly motivated by fear of the unknown. Second, when the disciples heard the news, they ran to confirm what Mary had reported. Their haste would have been motivated by the hope of Jesus' resurrection.

Mary's Experience at the Grave (20:2–10)

Mary made a second trip to the tomb. This time she was accompanied by two of the disciples, Simon Peter and the one the Gospel writer has chosen not to name. John records only that this "other disciple" was the one "whom Jesus loved" (John 20:2). The traditional view is that this disciple was the Apostle John.

The "other disciple" was the first to look into the tomb. Without going inside, he noticed the strips of linen lying there (20:4–5). Afterward, Simon Peter went straight into the tomb. He also noticed the position of the linen strips and the head covering (20:6–7). Then "the other disciple . . . also entered" (20:8).

John's Gospel keys in on a nuance of the story that gave the disciples a possible explanation of the absence of Jesus' body. John focuses our attention on the linen cloths in which Jesus was originally buried. The disciples understood the nature of these cloths being left behind. For them, the fact that the cloths were left behind was a sign that the body was not stolen. Tomb robbers would be moving in haste to dispose of the body. Therefore, it is unlikely that thieves would have taken the time to meticulously undo the tightly wound linens that covered Jesus' body.

When Jesus raised Lazarus from the dead, John 11:44 states, "The man who had died came forth, bound hand and foot with wrappings, and his face was wrapped around with a cloth. Jesus said to them, 'Unbind him, and let him go.'" Lazarus could not loose himself. He needed the assistance of some friends to untangle him. Jesus' body was wrapped in the same fashion.

No one was an eyewitness to the actual resurrection. We can only make some assumptions based on the evidence the Scriptures give. One assumption is that Jesus had divine assistance to be released from his grave clothes, an idea made plausible by the presence of the two angels at the tomb mentioned in verse 12. Another assumption is to believe that

Jesus' body was transfigured through the linen cloths and head covering so as to leave the cloths lying in their original form and place.

Verse 8 tells us, "So the other disciple who had come first to the tomb then also entered, and he saw and believed." The word translated "believed" describes the action of a person who is thoroughly convinced of something. The disciple based his belief on what he saw and experienced at the tomb, not the knowledge of Old Testament prophecy (20:9).

Mary's Encounter with Jesus (20:11–16)

Obviously some time passed between the disciples leaving the tomb and Mary encountering the risen Jesus. Verse 10 tells us that the disciples left to go "to their own homes." Mary was at the tomb feeling distraught.

Then Mary "stooped and looked into the tomb" (20:11). Verse 12 says, "she saw two angels in white sitting, one at the head and the other at the feet, where the body of Jesus had been lying." As she continued to cry out of the sorrow of her heart, the angels asked, "Woman, why are you weeping?" (20:13).

This question probably was spoken to console Mary and calm her fears. God in his providential care provided the presence of the angels

SPREADING THE GOOD NEWS

Mary and the two disciples running to the grave are examples of the Apostle Paul's message in Romans 10:15, as follows: "How will they preach unless they are sent? Just as it is written, HOW BEAUTIFUL ARE THE FEET OF THOSE WHO BRING GOOD NEWS OF GOOD THINGS!" The Greek word translated "preach" is the word kerusso, meaning to be a herald. A herald was one who proclaimed an important message usually on behalf of a magistrate. Heralds were the town criers, moving hastily from town to town, announcing good news. Notice how Paul mentioned "THE FEET OF THOSE WHO BRING GOOD NEWS." In ancient literature heralds are portrayed as runners.

A Christian does not have to be a preacher in order to act as a herald. As born-again believers in Jesus Christ, we must follow the example of Mary Magdalene in exercising expediency in telling others the good news of Jesus Christ's resurrection.

for Mary's sake. He knew that Mary, due to her devotion to Jesus, was not ready to witness an empty tomb alone. In like manner, Christians must act as encouragers to those who have lost loved ones dear to them, serving as a source of comfort and support.

Mary answered, "Because they have taken away my Lord, and I do not know where they have laid Him" (20:13). Mary used the word "they" in a general sense even though she did not know who had taken the body. Mary's unequivocal love for Jesus is heard in her voice as she referred to Jesus as "my Lord." The word "Lord" is used to describe the relationship one has with a person to whom much respect and reverence is given.

It was then that Mary was met by Jesus, although she did not readily recognize him. In verse 15 Mary addressed Jesus as "the gardener." She said, "Sir, if you have carried Him away, tell me where you have laid Him, and I will take Him away" (20:15).

Why did Mary not recognize Jesus? Several possible explanations can be derived. First, Mary might not have seen the full image of Jesus because of her tears. Another explanation would be that Mary's attention was not fully fixed on Jesus but on the empty tomb and the two angels inside. Then there is the blinding power of a fixed thought. Mary was so overwhelmed with grief, so pre-occupied with death, that she could not see life staring at her. The thought of the possibility that this voice speaking to her could be that of her living Savior did not enter her mind.

Jesus quelled her fears by simply calling her name, "Mary!" (20:16). When Mary heard her name, she recognized the familiar sound of Jesus' voice. As John 10:27 states, "My sheep hear My voice, and I know them, and they follow Me." Notice the contrast between Mary's faith and that of "the other disciple" in John 20:8. The other disciple believed based on what he saw. Mary believed based on what she heard. Romans 10:17 teaches us, "faith comes by hearing, and hearing by the word of God" (New King James Version). Mary responded to Jesus' voice with an exuberant "Rabboni!" She was expressing her joy that Jesus is alive.

Mary's Exciting News (20:17–18)

In Mary's excitement she evidently began to embrace Jesus. Jesus responded to Mary in verse 17, saying, "Stop clinging to Me, for I have not yet ascended to the Father." The Greek word translated "clinging," *haptou*, means *to fasten oneself to or to hold on to*. Apparently Mary grabbed hold of Jesus and acted as though she would not release him.

There has been much debate amongst Bible scholars over the meaning of Jesus' command to Mary not to hold on to him. The challenge is not to over-theologize this statement. Mary's outer posture demonstrated an inner desire for Jesus never to depart again. Jesus was explaining to her that his physical presence with them would be limited, for he had to ascend to the Father. It does not mean, as some have suggested, that Jesus' resurrected body was untouchable.

Jesus spoke to Mary regarding his ascension. This is a critical element of the gospel story, one that shapes our entire belief system as a Christian community of faith. We affirm by faith that Jesus Christ was crucified, dead, buried, and resurrected on the morning of the third day. This same Jesus, after forty days of appearing to certain of his followers, "ascended," or *was lifted up* to heaven to be with the Father. Detailed accounts of Jesus' ascension are given in Luke 24:50–53 and Acts 1:6–11. It is important to note that these accounts agree with each other, even though the account in Acts provides more details.

The tense of the Greek verb translated "ascending" indicates it was an action that was happening at that time. The word is in the present tense. What Jesus was communicating to Mary was to make haste and tell the disciples, whom Jesus referred to as "My brethren," that he had not ascended yet but the process had begun and would not delay. The use of "My Father and your Father, and My God and your God" in the latter part of verse 17 proclaimed to Mary that he was about to take his rightful place at the right side of God the Father.

Mary Magdalene received her commission from the Lord in verse 17. In verse 18 she became the first post-resurrection evangelist by carrying the good news to the disciples. Her joy was wrapped up in one simple statement: "I have seen the Lord!"

Implications and Actions

God fashioned the events on that first Easter morning in such a way as to stir a joyous excitement in the hearts of those who would tell the story. That society depended on the eyewitness accounts of events being passed verbally. How tragic it would have been if Mary and the disciples had kept this news to themselves. The joy of knowing Jesus is alive propelled them to share the good news with everyone.

Are you willing to share the gospel of Jesus Christ with a lost world? As we celebrate the resurrection of Jesus on this Easter, let us reflect on the remarkable task we have as Christians to tell others the good news of salvation in Jesus Christ.

QUESTIONS

1. Describe in your own words the emotions Mary must have felt when she first reached the tomb and found it empty. How did this experience change her life?

2. In what ways can Mary Magdalene's actions help you further the gospel?

3. What are some reasons a Christian would be hesitant to share the gospel?

4. How can one get past these reasons and actually share the gospel?

NOTES ──

1. Unless otherwise indicated, all Scripture quotations in "Introducing Psalms: Songs from the Heart of Faith," lesson 3, and the Easter lesson are from the New American Standard Bible (1995 edition).

2. See Raymond E. Brown, *The Gospel According to John*, The Anchor Bible, vol. 29a (Garden City, NY: Doubleday & Company, Inc.), 844, 980.

Our Next New Study
(Available for use beginning June 2013)

Guidance for the Seasons of Life

Lesson 1	Daniel and His Friends: Opting for Faithfulness	Daniel 1
Lesson 2	Samson: Realizing You're Not Indestructible	Judges 16:4–30
Lesson 3	Joseph: Gaining Maturity	Genesis 37:2–14, 18–28; 39:1–12
Lesson 4	Rebekah: Finding Love	Genesis 24:34–67
Lesson 5	Hannah: Praying for a Child	1 Samuel 1:1–20
Lesson 6	Ruth: Finding Love After Loss	Ruth 1:1–19a; 3:6–13; 4:13–17
Lesson 7	Joseph: Using Abilities to Serve Others	Genesis 41:25–57; 45:4–8
Lesson 8	Caleb: Offering Wise and Courageous Leadership	Numbers 13:1–2, 17–33; Joshua 14:6–10
Lesson 9	Joseph: Living in the Middle	Genesis 47:27—48:2, 8–19; 49:33—50:6
Lesson 10	David: Overwhelmed By Family Turmoil	2 Samuel 13:1–2, 20–22, 30–37; 14:21–24; 15:7–14; 18:6–15, 33
Lesson 11	Samuel: Transitioning from Leadership	1 Samuel 8:1–10; 12:1–5

Lesson 12   Moses: Dying Well   Deuteronomy 34
Lesson 13   Reaching the Highest Point of   1 Corinthians 15:3–20,
                    Human Life   35–44, 50–57

How to Order More Bible Study Materials

It's easy! Just fill in the following information. For additional Bible study materials available both in print and online, see www.baptistwaypress.org, or get a complete order form of available print materials—including Spanish materials—by calling 1-866-249-1799 or e-mailing baptistway@texasbaptists.org.

Title of item	Price	Quantity	Cost
This Issue:			
Psalms: Songs from the Heart of Faith—Study Guide (BWP001152)	$3.95	_____	_____
Psalms: Songs from the Heart of Faith—Large Print Study Guide (BWP001153)	$4.25	_____	_____
Psalms: Songs from the Heart of Faith—Teaching Guide (BWP001154)	$4.95	_____	_____
Additional Issues Available:			
Growing Together in Christ—Study Guide (BWP001036)	$3.25	_____	_____
Growing Together in Christ—Teaching Guide (BWP001038)	$3.75	_____	_____
Living Generously for Jesus' Sake—Study Guide (BWP001137)	$3.95	_____	_____
Living Generously for Jesus' Sake—Large Print Study Guide (BWP001138)	$4.25	_____	_____
Living Generously for Jesus' Sake—Teaching Guide (BWP001139)	$4.95	_____	_____
Living Faith in Daily Life—Study Guide (BWP001095)	$3.55	_____	_____
Living Faith in Daily Life—Large Print Study Guide (BWP001096)	$3.95	_____	_____
Living Faith in Daily Life—Teaching Guide (BWP001097)	$4.25	_____	_____
Participating in God's Mission—Study Guide (BWP001077)	$3.55	_____	_____
Participating in God's Mission—Large Print Study Guide (BWP001078)	$3.95	_____	_____
Participating in God's Mission—Teaching Guide (BWP001079)	$3.95	_____	_____
Profiles in Character—Study Guide (BWP001112)	$3.55	_____	_____
Profiles in Character—Large Print Study Guide (BWP001113)	$4.25	_____	_____
Profiles in Character—Teaching Guide (BWP001114)	$4.95	_____	_____
Genesis: People Relating to God—Study Guide (BWP001088)	$2.35	_____	_____
Genesis: People Relating to God—Large Print Study Guide (BWP001089)	$2.75	_____	_____
Genesis: People Relating to God—Teaching Guide (BWP001090)	$2.95	_____	_____
Ezra, Haggai, Zechariah, Nehemiah, Malachi—Study Guide (BWP001071)	$3.25	_____	_____
Ezra, Haggai, Zechariah, Nehemiah, Malachi—Large Print Study Guide (BWP001072)	$3.55	_____	_____
Ezra, Haggai, Zechariah, Nehemiah, Malachi—Teaching Guide (BWP001073)	$3.75	_____	_____
Amos. Hosea, Isaiah, Micah: Calling for Justice, Mercy, and Faithfulness—Study Guide (BWP001132)	$3.95	_____	_____
Amos. Hosea, Isaiah, Micah: Calling for Justice, Mercy, and Faithfulness—Large Print Study Guide (BWP001133)	$4.25	_____	_____
Amos. Hosea, Isaiah, Micah: Calling for Justice, Mercy, and Faithfulness—Teaching Guide (BWP001134)	$4.95	_____	_____
The Gospel of Matthew: A Primer for Discipleship—Study Guide (BWP001127)	$3.95	_____	_____
The Gospel of Matthew: A Primer for Discipleship—Large Print Study Guide (BWP001128)	$4.25	_____	_____
The Gospel of Matthew: A Primer for Discipleship—Teaching Guide (BWP001129)	$4.95	_____	_____
Matthew: Hope in the Resurrected Christ—Study Guide (BWP001066)	$3.25	_____	_____
Matthew: Hope in the Resurrected Christ—Large Print Study Guide (BWP001067)	$3.55	_____	_____
Matthew: Hope in the Resurrected Christ—Teaching Guide (BWP001068)	$3.75	_____	_____
The Gospel of Mark: People Responding to Jesus—Study Guide (BWP001147)	$3.95	_____	_____
The Gospel of Mark: People Responding to Jesus—Large Print Study Guide (BWP001148)	$4.25	_____	_____
The Gospel of Mark: People Responding to Jesus—Teaching Guide (BWP001149)	$4.95	_____	_____
The Gospel of John: Light Overcoming Darkness, Part One—Study Guide (BWP001104)	$3.55	_____	_____
The Gospel of John: Light Overcoming Darkness, Part One—Large Print Study Guide (BWP001105)	$3.95	_____	_____
The Gospel of John: Light Overcoming Darkness, Part One—Teaching Guide (BWP001106)	$4.50	_____	_____
The Gospel of John: Light Overcoming Darkness, Part Two—Study Guide (BWP001109)	$3.55	_____	_____
The Gospel of John: Light Overcoming Darkness, Part Two—Large Print Study Guide (BWP001110)	$3.95	_____	_____
The Gospel of John: Light Overcoming Darkness, Part Two—Teaching Guide (BWP001111)	$4.50	_____	_____
The Book of Acts: Time to Act on Acts 1:8—Study Guide (BWP001142)	$3.95	_____	_____
The Book of Acts: Time to Act on Acts 1:8—Large Print Study Guide (BWP001143)	$4.25	_____	_____
The Book of Acts: Time to Act on Acts 1:8—Teaching Guide (BWP001144)	$4.95	_____	_____
The Corinthian Letters—Study Guide (BWP001121)	$3.55	_____	_____
The Corinthian Letters—Large Print Study Guide (BWP001122)	$4.25	_____	_____
The Corinthian Letters—Teaching Guide (BWP001123)	$4.95	_____	_____

Galatians and 1&2 Thessalonians—Study Guide (BWP001080)	$3.55	_____	_____
Galatians and 1&2 Thessalonians—Large Print Study Guide (BWP001081)	$3.95	_____	_____
Galatians and 1&2 Thessalonians—Teaching Guide (BWP001082)	$3.95	_____	_____
Letters of James and John—Study Guide (BWP001101)	$3.55	_____	_____
Letters of James and John—Large Print Study Guide (BWP001102)	$3.95	_____	_____
Letters of James and John—Teaching Guide (BWP001103)	$4.25	_____	_____

Coming for use beginning June 2013

Guidance for the Seasons of Life—Study Guide (BWP001157)	$3.95	_____	_____
Guidance for the Seasons of Life—Large Print Study Guide (BWP001158)	$4.25	_____	_____
Guidance for the Seasons of Life—Teaching Guide (BWP001159)	$4.95	_____	_____

Cost
of items (Order value)   _____

Shipping charges
(see chart*)   _____

TOTAL   _____

Standard (UPS/Mail) Shipping Charges*			
Order Value	Shipping charge**	Order Value	Shipping charge**
$.01—$9.99	$6.50	$160.00—$199.99	$24.00
$10.00—$19.99	$8.50	$200.00—$249.99	$28.00
$20.00—$39.99	$9.50	$250.00—$299.99	$30.00
$40.00—$59.99	$10.50	$300.00—$349.99	$34.00
$60.00—$79.99	$11.50	$350.00—$399.99	$42.00
$80.00—$99.99	$12.50	$400.00—$499.99	$50.00
$100.00—$129.99	$15.00	$500.00—$599.99	$60.00
$130.00—$159.99	$20.00	$600.00—$799.99	$72.00**

*Plus, applicable taxes for individuals and other taxable entities (not churches) within Texas will be added. Please call 1-866-249-1799 if the exact amount is needed prior to ordering.

**For order values $800.00 and above, please call 1-866-249-1799 or check www.baptistwaypress.org

Please allow three weeks for standard delivery. For express shipping service: Call 1-866-249-1799 for information on additional charges.

YOUR NAME _____ PHONE _____

YOUR CHURCH _____ DATE ORDERED _____

SHIPPING ADDRESS _____

CITY _____ STATE _____ ZIP CODE _____

E-MAIL _____

MAIL this form with your check for the total amount to
BAPTISTWAY PRESS, Baptist General Convention of Texas,
333 North Washington, Dallas, TX 75246-1798
(Make checks to "Baptist Executive Board.")

OR, **FAX** your order anytime to: 214-828-5376, and we will bill you.

OR, **CALL** your order toll-free: 1-866-249-1799
(M-Fri 8:30 a.m.-5:00 p.m. central time), and we will bill you.

OR, **E-MAIL** your order to our internet e-mail address:
baptistway@texasbaptists.org, and we will bill you.

OR, **ORDER ONLINE** at www.baptistwaypress.org.

We look forward to receiving your order! Thank you!